CW00410323

/

20
Mysteries
of the
Rosary
A Scriptural Journey

ROSARY PRAYERS INCLUDED

M. Basil Pennington, O.C.S.O.

Liguori
LIGUORI, MISSOURI

Imprimi Potest: Richard Thibodeau, C.Ss.R. • Provincial, Denver Province • The Redemptorists

Published by Liguori Publications • Liguori, Missouri
www.liguori.org
www.catholicbooksonline.com

Library of Congress Cataloging-in-Publication Data

Pennington, M. Basil.
    Twenty mysteries of the Rosary : a scriptural journey / M. Basil Pennington.
       p. cm.
    ISBN 0-7648-1100-2
    1. Rosary. 2. Mysteries of the Rosary. I. Title.

BX2163.P46 2003
242'.74—dc21   2003052798

This book is revised edition of both *The Fifteen Mysteries: In Image and Word,* published in 1993 by Our Sunday Visitor Publishing Division, Huntington, Indiana, and *Praying by Hand: Rediscovering the Rosary As a Way of Prayer*, published in 1991 by HarperSanFrancisco, San Francisco, California.

Printed in the United States of America
07 06 05 04 03   5 4 3 2 1
First edition

For Neal in friendship.

Contents

Welcome

I have to smile every time I think of it. My first book on Centering Prayer, *Daily We Touch Him*, had just been published. I sent a copy of it to my aunt. I was eager to get her reaction to it. Aunt Marion was quite a woman, the highest paid woman in AT&T at that time. After she had time to read the book, I anxiously inquired as to her appreciation of it. Aunt Marion said it was a good book, clear and simple; it would help many. And then she added: But I will stick with the rosary!

Certainly, devotion to Mary and to the rosary was a part of my life from the beginning, in our family, in our home. My earliest memories of the experience of God come with images of sitting in church next to my grandmother praying her beads. To the day they were placed in her hands as she lay in her coffin, they were never far from her hands, those hands so worn by loving labor for us all. And the same could be said of my mother.

In years past I have written two books on the rosary: *Praying by Hand: Rediscovering the Rosary As a Way of Prayer* and *The Fifteen Mysteries: In Image and Word*. This present volume gathers up sections from both these previous books, and adds something new: we now have twenty mysteries.

Pope John Paul II has given us not only five new mysteries, the Mysteries of Light, but in his Apostolic Letter "*Rosarium Virginis Mariae*" ("The Rosary of the Virgin Mary"), he has given us a rich spiritual theology of this wonderful practice of prayer, a way of prayer which is truly Christocentric. Following his predecessors, he sees the rosary as a "compendium" of the Gospel, containing "all the light of the Gospel message in its entirety" ("Rosary," 1). We sit "at the school of Mary" ("Rosary," 1) and learn "to contemplate the beauty on the face of Christ and to experience the depths of his love. It is not just a question of learning what he taught but of *learning him*" ("Rosary," 1, 14). How beautifully and richly the pope develops his reflections on Mary's contemplation of her son and relates it with our experience in the liturgy. The whole of this inspiring letter deserves not only to be read more than once, it deserves to be studied.

It can be found on the Vatican Web page: www.vatican.va.

In the course of this volume, I include some of the pope's concise reflections on the mysteries, but there is much more to be found in his pastoral letter. For me, one of the striking elements of it is the pope's sensitivity to the current ecumenical and interreligious climate. Noting "contemporary culture, even amid so many indications to the contrary, has witnessed the flowering of a new call for spirituality," he goes on to say this is "due also to the influence of other religions" ("Rosary," 5). He argues: "If properly revitalized, the Rosary is an aid and certainly not a hindrance to ecumenism!" ("Rosary," 4). It is "a devotion directed to the Christological center of the Christian faith, in such a way that 'when the Mother is honored, the Son…is duly known, loved and glorified'" ("Rosary," 4).

John Paul II is not outside of history in his thinking. Pointing to "the terrifying attacks of September 11, 2001" ("Rosary," 6) he looks to the rosary as a desperately needed prayer for peace. Still more profoundly in touch with the needs of our times, the pope explores the "anthropological significance of the Rosary" ("Rosary," 25). "Anyone who contemplates Christ through the various stages of his life cannot fail to perceive in him *the truth about man [and woman]*" ("Rosary," 25). He goes on to develop this: "Contemplating Christ's birth, they learn of the sanctity of life; seeing the household of Nazareth, they learn the original truth of the family according to God's plan; listening to the Master in the mysteries of his public ministry, they find the light which leads them to enter the Kingdom of God; and following him on the way to Calvary, they learn the meaning of salvific suffering. Finally, contemplating Christ and his Blessed Mother in glory, they see the goal towards which each of us is called, if we allow ourselves to be healed and transformed by Holy Spirit" ("Rosary," 25). In fact, this pope makes this bold statement: "To understand the Rosary, one has to enter into the psychological dynamic proper to love" ("Rosary," 26). While it is true that "Christian spirituality is familiar with the most sublime forms of mystical silence in which images, words and gestures are all, so to speak, superseded by an intense and ineffable union with God, it normally engages the whole person in all his [or her] complex psychological, physical and relational reality" ("Rosary," 27).

Defining Christian spirituality as "the

disciple's commitment to become conformed ever more fully to his [or her] Master" ("Rosary," 15), the pope notes: "In the spiritual journey of the Rosary, based on the constant contemplation—in Mary's company—of the face of Christ, this demanding ideal of being conformed to him is pursued through an association which could be described in terms of friendship…. The cycles of meditation proposed by the Holy Rosary are by no means exhaustive, but they do bring to mind what is essential and they awaken in the soul a thirst for a knowledge of Christ continually nourished by the pure source of the Gospel" ("Rosary," 15). The pope wants the rosary to be "a true doorway to the depths of the Heart of Christ, ocean of joy and of light, of suffering and of glory" ("Rosary," 19). Quoting Saint Paul's heartfelt prayer for all the baptized in his letter to the Ephesians, "I pray that…Christ may dwell in your hearts through faith, as you are being rooted and grounded in love. I pray that you may have the power…to know the love of Christ that surpasses knowledge, so that you may be filled with all the fullness of God" (3:16, 17–19), the pope adds quite simply: "The Rosary is at the service of this ideal" ("Rosary," 24).

In developing his practical teaching on the

use of this "method of contemplation," the pope asserts: "The Rosary is no substitute for *lectio divina*; on the contrary, it presupposes and promotes it" ("Rosary," 29). And he suggests: "In order to supply a Biblical foundation and greater depth to our meditation, it is helpful to follow the announcement of the mystery with *the proclamation of a related biblical passage*, long or short, depending on the circumstances" ("Rosary," 30). In service of this we place before each meditation some appropriate Scripture, usually that cited by the pope in his Apostolic Letter. The further guidance of the pope in regards to these words is also worth listening to: "No other words can ever match the efficacy of the inspired word. As we listen, we are certain that this is the word of God, spoken for today and spoken 'for me.' It is not a matter of recalling information but of *allowing God to speak*" ("Rosary," 30).

The meditations I offer here are quite short. Certainly, I could write a whole book on each of these mysteries. But what is offered here is meant to simply open space for your own thoughts and memories, affections and imaginations, to bring you into the experience of the mystery and its meaning in your life today, at this moment, where you are right now.

As a Trappist abbot I would especially like to endorse these words of the pope:

Listening and meditation are nourished by silence. After the announcement of the mystery and the proclamation of the word, it is fitting to pause and focus one's attention for a suitable period of time on the mystery concerned, before moving into vocal prayer. A discovery of the importance of silence is one of the secrets of practicing contemplation and meditation. One drawback of a society dominated by technology and the mass media is the fact that silence becomes increasingly difficult to achieve. Just as moments of silence are recommended in the Liturgy, so too in the recitation of the Rosary it is fitting to pause briefly after listening to the word of God, while the mind focuses on the content of a particular mystery ("Rosary," 31).

As I said above, the whole of the pope's beautiful, profound, and practical letter, which invites us to an enriched life lifted up by contemplative prayer, deserves to be read and reread. Let me simply conclude with his words: "A prayer so easy and yet so rich truly deserves to be rediscovered by the Christian community…. I look to all of you, brothers and sisters of every state of life, to you, Christian families, to you, the sick and elderly, and to you, young people: *confidently take up the Rosary once again.* Rediscover the Rosary in the light of Scripture, in harmony with the Liturgy, and in the context of your daily lives" ("Rosary," 43).

+ M. Basil
Feast of Our Lady of Lourdes
February 11, 2003

How to Pray the Rosary

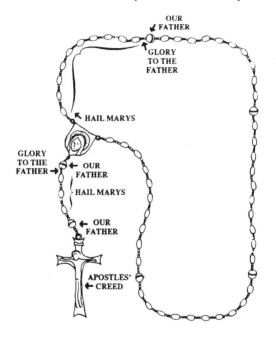

OUR FATHER

GLORY TO THE FATHER

HAIL MARYS

GLORY TO THE FATHER

OUR FATHER

HAIL MARYS

OUR FATHER

APOSTLES' CREED

W e begin by making the Sign of the Cross. Then we say the Apostles' Creed, one Our Father, three Hail Marys, and one Glory to the Father (Prayer of Praise) on the small chain.

Next recall the first mystery and contemplate that mystery (with or without the assistance of the reflections provided herein).

Say one Our Father, ten Hail Marys, and one Glory Be to the Father. This completes one decade. All the other decades are said in the same manner with a different mystery meditated upon during each decade.

At the end of the rosary, the prayer Hail, Holy Queen may be recited.

The new pattern suggested by Pope John Paul II indicates also the distribution of the mysteries during the week, as follows:

The Joyful Mysteries	Monday & Saturday
The Mysteries of Light	Thursday
The Sorrowful Mysteries	Tuesday & Friday
The Glorious Mysteries	Wednesday & Sunday

The Prayers of the Rosary

The Sign of the Cross

In the name of the Father, and of the Son, and of Holy Spirit. Amen.

The Apostles' Creed

I believe in God, the Father almighty, creator of heaven and earth. I believe in Jesus Christ, his only Son, our Lord. He was conceived by the Holy Spirit and born of the Virgin Mary. He suffered under Pontius Pilate, was crucified, died, and was buried. He descended to the dead. On the third day he rose again. He ascended into heaven and is seated at the right hand of the Father. He will come to judge the living and the dead. I believe in the Holy Spirit, the holy catholic Church, the communion of saints, the forgiveness of sins, the resurrection of the body, and the life everlasting. Amen.

Our Father
(The Lord's Prayer)

> Our Father, who art in heaven, hallowed be thy name; thy kingdom come; thy will be done on earth as it is in heaven. Give us this day our daily bread; and forgive us our trespasses as we forgive those who trespass against us; lead us not into temptation, but deliver us from evil. Amen.

Hail Mary
(The Angelic Salutation)

> Hail, Mary, full of grace! The Lord is with you; blessed are you among women, and blessed is the fruit of your womb, Jesus. Holy Mary, Mother of God, pray for us sinners now and at the hour of our death. Amen.

Glory Be to the Father
(The Doxology)

> Glory be to the Father, and to the Son, and to Holy Spirit. As it was in the beginning, is now, and ever shall be, world without end. Amen.

Hail, Holy Queen
(Salve Regina)

Hail, holy Queen, Mother of Mercy; hail our life, our sweetness, and our hope. To you do we cry, poor banished children of Eve. To you do we send up our sighs, mourning and weeping in this valley of tears.

Turn, then, most gracious advocate, your eyes of mercy toward us. And after this our exile show unto us the blessed fruit of your womb, Jesus. O clement, O loving, O sweet Virgin Mary.

Pray for us, O holy Mother of God, that we may be made worthy of the promises of Christ.

Let us pray.

Pour forth, we beseech you, O Lord, your grace into our hearts, that we to whom the incarnation of Christ your Son was made known by the message of an angel, may by his passion and cross be brought to the glory of his resurrection, through the same Christ, our Lord. Amen.

20
Mysteries
of the
Rosary

The Five
Joyful
Mysteries

The first five decades, the "joyful mysteries," are marked by the joy radiating from the event of the Incarnation. This is clear from the very first mystery.... To meditate upon the "joyful" mysteries, then, is to enter into the ultimate causes and the deepest meaning of Christian joy. It is to focus on the realism of the mystery of the Incarnation and on the obscure foreshadowing of the mystery of the saving Passion. Mary leads us to discover the secret of Christian joy, reminding us that Christianity is, first and foremost, evangelism, "good news," which has as its heart and its whole content the person of Jesus Christ, the Word made flesh, the one Savior of the world.

"APOSTOLIC LETTER OF POPE JOHN PAUL II
ON THE MOST HOLY ROSARY:
ROSARIUM VIRGINIS MARIAE," 20

The First Joyful Mystery

The Annunciation

In the sixth month the angel Gabriel was sent by God to a town in Galilee called Nazareth, to a virgin engaged to a man whose name was Joseph, of the house of David. The virgin's name was Mary. And he came to her and said, "Greetings, favored one! The Lord is with you." But she was much perplexed by his words and pondered what sort of greeting this might be. The angel said to her, "Do not be afraid, Mary, for you have found favor with God. And now, you will conceive in your womb and bear a son, and you will name him Jesus. He will be great, and will be called the Son of the Most High, and the Lord God will give to him the throne of his ancestor David. He will reign over the house of Jacob forever, and of his kingdom there will be no end." Mary said to the angel, "How can this be, since I am a virgin?" The angel said to her, "The Holy Spirit will come upon you, and the power of the Most High will overshadow you; therefore the child to be born will be holy; he will be called Son of God. And now, your relative Elizabeth in her old age has also conceived a son; and this is the sixth month for her who was said to be barren. For nothing will be impossible with God." Then Mary said, "Here am I, the servant of the Lord; let it be with me according to your word." Then the angel departed from her.

LUKE 1:26–38

The Basilica at the Annunciation (in Nazareth) is a good place to begin. A church built on many levels, it contains homes from the time of Jesus, an early Christian place of worship, a Constantinian basilica, the enormous basilica of the Crusaders, and today's strikingly modern edifice, which rises above all its surroundings. The event that traditionally took place here has drawn forth the talents of every succeeding age. Men and women of great talent have expressed their meditations on this mystery in stone, mosaic, and paint, uncovering the many levels of the mystery itself. As I sit here writing, groups of pilgrims pass by speaking the languages of many nations. This mystery belongs to all people of all times, each assimilating and living it in his or her own way according to each ones particular grace.

I sit opposite the little grotto that traditionally covers the site of the home of Joachim and Anne. Beneath the altar, pilgrims bend to kiss the marble stone: *Hic Verbum caro factum est.* "Here the Word was made flesh."

I am a bit weary from the long, hot journey. Things did not all go as I would have liked, so I have some remaining feelings of anger, self-pity, and hurt. How out of place these all seem in the face of this awesome mystery: God coming to us in our very own humanity. But this is what it is all about. He became one of us, like us in all but sin yet taking on even our sin so that he could heal all of this. If I am to give him my humanity, it has to be this poor, needy, weak, and sinful humanity. There is no other "me" to offer him now. It is crazy to think that we have to get all spruced up to offer ourselves to God.

in fact, the only way we *can* get spruced up is by offering our mess to him.

One of the wonders of what took place here—and in sacramental mystery continues to take place here—is that one of us had a humanity to give him that was *not* messed up. But that was so only because, in a way that it took us a long time to understand, he "spruced up" Mary's humanity at the very instant it became hers.

I wonder, though, if Mary was not more conscious of unworthiness than we unworthy sinners are. Did not this little woman—barely more than a girl—who had faithfully pondered the Scriptures through the years and entered into the liturgies and rituals of her people come to a deep sense of the awesomeness of Yahweh? Surely God had prepared Mary in a special way for this moment. Without some divine illumination she could never have grasped the angelic message sufficiently to give human assent. Yet any illumination concerning the Trinity—the fact that Yahweh is three in one, a Father who has a Son who by the action of their Holy Spirit will become in a completely human, physical way *her* son—must have made Yahweh even more awesome. "Mary, do not be afraid." Yet how fearsome is this mystery!

And how loving! For love is the whole motive and message.

Mary was familiar enough with angels, or at least with the idea of angels. She had been nurtured on the Scriptures. And the Scriptures are full of angels. The Scriptures are not too descriptive in presenting them. They evidently did take on some sort of human form. Three—were they angels or the Trinity itself?—came to Abraham and Sarah to announce another miraculous birth. Unbeknown to Mary, only a few months before one of the heavenly messengers stood at the right hand of the altar of incense in the Temple at Jerusalem and told Zechariah of another miraculous conception—like Abraham and Sarah's, a miracle of old age, yet one intimately connected with this very young virgin.

The angel points to what is above, beyond all our everyday experience; indeed, beyond what our poor minds can fully grasp, to most sublime mystery, to what eye has not seen nor ear heard, nor has it even entered into the human mind.

Mary had grown up within and been fully formed by a people who had been able to keep their proper sense as a unique and chosen people because they cherished the precious revelation that God is one and unique, Yahweh. There is no God but our God. Listen, O Israel, your God is one God, the only true God.

Now, suddenly, not only is Mary confronted with the appearance of an angel—as frightening, awesome, and troublesome as that might be—but this angel tells her Yahweh has a son. And what is more, she is to be the mother of that son. What is a twelve-year-old Jewish girl to do with that?

Mary had already matured much. She had gone through a very extraordinary and graced discernment. And she had drawn another into it, the man she was betrothed to marry. Despite the Lord's command to increase and multiply and the universal Jewish response to that command, Mary had discerned a unique call to live in a virginal marriage. Was she all wrong? She only wanted to do God's will.

But this was not a question of an ordinary maternity. The angel pointed to something unfathomably sublime. A divine pregnancy. A virginal pregnancy. Didn't this belong to the mythology of the pagans who conquered and sought to seduce the Jews? This was real. Grace abounded in this encounter. There was no doubt in the authenticity of this message and messenger. Only the inconceivability of a divine conceiving.

Mary had no concepts, no images, which could embrace the reality that was being revealed to her. She could only give herself, follow the direction of the angel, and let mystery descend upon her and expand her whole being, filling it with the divine at every level of being. Her only answer could be: "Let it happen to me"—a totally active passivity. A being that said a complete and unbounded "yes" to God, to let the divine bring forth the inconceivable within her through a divine conception.

Like Mary, we can only allow the fullness of the mystery abide with us, letting it form us, raising us to a new, unheard of, inconceivable sublimity.

For in the Incarnation, not only does God become man—human, but the human, a man becomes God. And all humanity is summoned to divinity. The angel points for us, too, to what is above, beyond everything we can conceive. God became man in order that man—and woman—might become divine—true partakers of the divine nature and life. What can we do with this inconceivable concept?

Like Mary, we can only say our own *Fiat*. Let

it happen to me according to your word, your plan, your will.

The angel, with all the dynamism of her being, invites us to go beyond. Word and gesture, eye and finger, invite us to transcend. No thoughts are too sublime for us—if only we remember it is a divine invitation. It is all gift. Ours is but to receive. To wholly receive, to put no limits on our receiving, to hang on to none of our own limitations. To let God be God in us and bring us into a whole new level of being. Let it happen to me.

Our Father…

The Second Joyful Mystery

The Visitation

In those days Mary set out and went with haste to a Judean town in the hill country, where she entered the house of Zechariah and greeted Elizabeth. When Elizabeth heard Mary's greeting, the child leaped in her womb. And Elizabeth was filled with the Holy Spirit and exclaimed with a loud cry, "Blessed are you among women, and blessed is the fruit of your womb. And why has this happened to me, that the mother of my Lord comes to me? For as soon as I heard the sound of your greeting, the child in my womb leaped for joy. And blessed is she who believed that there would be a fulfillment of what was spoken to her by the Lord."

And Mary said,
"My soul magnifies the Lord,
    and my spirit rejoices in God
        my Savior,

for he has looked with favor on the
lowliness of his servant.
Surely, from now on all
generations will call
me blessed;
for the Mighty One has done great
things for me,
and holy is his name.
His mercy is for those who fear him
from generation to generation.
He has shown strength with
his arm;
he has scattered the proud in the
thoughts of their hearts.
He has brought down the powerful
from their thrones,
and lifted up the lowly;
he has filled the hungry with
good things,
and sent the rich away empty.
He has helped his servant Israel,
in remembrance of his mercy,
according to the promise he made
to our ancestors,
to Abraham and to his
descendants forever."

And Mary remained with her about three
months and then returned to her home.

LUKE 1:39–56

En Karem. Even today, in an air-conditioned
car, the journey from Nazareth to En Karem
(southeast of Jerusalem) is not an easy one:
heat, dust, the bleakness of desert and deso-
late land, and the pervasive sense of hostil-
ity in Samaria. All that has not changed much.
And even when one reaches the village, the
journey is not over. The church on the out-
skirts that stands on the site of the home of
Elizabeth and Zechariah is difficult to find,
nestled high on one of the ascents toward
Jerusalem.

But now I sit in the beautiful courtyard. Flowers of all sorts dance in the sunny breeze. Opposite me are the remains of the medieval church,
with a modern tower that reaches high over the
new sandstone church. Behind me on the wall
are ceramic plaques with Mary's *Magnificat* in
forty-four languages.

Mary's coming here was her first concrete expression of the faith she placed in God and in

his angel's message. And it is that faith that is magnified here. "Blessed is she who believed." Later Jesus, when a woman proclaimed his mother happy in bearing him, praised even more her faith.

Mary—she was like a beautiful cup of the finest gold, a ciborium set with the most precious stones and covered with a silken veil, hidden in the tabernacle and brought out only to bring the eucharistic Lord to others. Mary's life was so completely hidden.

We know little about it. When and where was she born? Who were her parents? The apocrypha tell delightful tales of her being presented in the Temple at Jerusalem when she was three. She danced on the steps of the Holy of Holies and gave joy to every heart. From that time she grew up within the sanctuary close to the holy place. Such fanciful things were hardly possible, though the site of Saint Anne's Church, which is said to cover her home, is very close to the temple precincts.

How her virginal marriage with Joseph, the just man from Nazareth, was arranged is also unknown to us. We only know she was betrothed to him and living in Nazareth when the angel came to ask her to be the mother of God.

She heard the message with an enlightened faith and said her wholehearted "yes."

The angel had told her of another special pregnancy, that of her aged cousin Elizabeth. It was not exactly meant to be a sign to Mary. Her faith did not need signs. It was more a word of comfort. And a call to comfort and assist the elderly woman in her hour.

With great courage Mary made the journey south. It took a lot of courage. What explanation did she give to her parents or guardians and to her espoused? She undoubtedly joined a pilgrim band or a merchant caravan that was heading for Jerusalem. The group probably did not dare to set out directly through alien Samaritan territory. The journey down along the river would be safer, but certainly longer and hotter. It would be a difficult journey for a young woman who was entering into the mystery of her first pregnancy and would not have any female confidant at her side to support her. All the while she must have wondered how things would be worked out with Joseph and her family. The future was full of awesome and fearful questions.

As she entered the courtyard of Zechariah's home, there was the elderly woman so obviously pregnant. Mary's cry of love reached receptive ears. Elizabeth all but leapt up herself, her face aglow:

> "Blessed are you among women, and blessed is the fruit of your womb. And why has this happened to me, that the mother of my Lord comes to me? For as soon as I heard the sound of your greeting, the child in my womb leaped for joy. And blessed is she who believed that there would be a fulfillment of what was spoken to her by the Lord" (Luke 1:42–45).

Yes, Elizabeth knew. And Mary's mission had begun.

Elizabeth knew. There was another with whom Mary could share her sublime secret. And all her fears and wonderment in their pregnancies. What days and weeks these two cousins must have had together. Even in that first moment of encounter, as they rushed into each other's arms, Mary could feel her son's cousin dancing for joy within his mother. The kick of life told her so much of what was to be. In how many ways was Elizabeth to assure her, enable her to foresee what was to come, help her to confidently trust that her son's Father would resolve all the difficulties with Joseph and the family.

And Mary's mission had begun. The mission which Mary would henceforth exercise, most times in hidden ways. She would be bringing Jesus, the Savior, her son and God's, to others— bringing his outpouring grace, his prophetic insight, his abounding joy. Mary had begun that mission which we speak of as we hail her as the mediatrix of all grace. At Cana we will get a glimpse of her active mediation. On Calvary we will see her intimate association with her son and hear the divine command that she is to mother all of us, the whole Christ. As Pentecost approaches, a fearful Church will be gathered around her in prayer. But for the most part hers will be a hidden service, a quiet ministry of prayer and love. It is only in these very first days of her ministry that God gives us a clear intimation as to what Mary's role is to be in the plan of salvation. She is to bring to each one of us our Savior with all his grace and joy.

We can understand Mary's role in our lives most fully, I think, if we envision our lives as being lived in the womb, in preparation to being born to eternal life. Christian tradition has always called the day of death the *dies natalis*, the day of birth, the day we are born to unending life. During the long gestation of this temporal life, which may well last nine decades, though probably less, Mary is mothering, nurturing, constantly channeling to us a participation in divine life and all that sustains such life in us. Through her ministry, as through a life cord, the graces are coming to us that will enable us to grow into a full Christ-person. Mary brings us Christ, our true joy, the source of all our life and hope. With this presence, even though we do not see and still live in faith in the darkness of the womb, we can, like John, leap and dance for joy.

Our Father…

The Third Joyful Mystery

The Birth of Jesus

In those days a decree went out from Emperor Augustus that all the world should be registered. This was the first registration and was taken while Quirinius was governor of Syria. All went to their own towns to be registered. Joseph also went from the town of Nazareth in Galilee to Judea, to the city of David called Bethlehem, because he was descended from the house and family of David. He went to be registered with Mary, to whom he was engaged and who was expecting a child. While they were there, the time came for her to deliver her child. And she gave birth to her firstborn son and wrapped him in bands of cloth, and laid him in a manger, because there was no place for them in the inn.

In that region there were shepherds living in the fields, keeping watch over their flock by night. Then an angel of the Lord stood before them, and the glory of the Lord shone around them, and they were terrified. But the angel said to them, "Do not be afraid; for see—I am bringing you good news of great joy for all the people: to you is born this day in the city of David a Savior, who is the Messiah, the Lord. This will be a sign for you: you will find a child wrapped in bands of cloth and lying in a manger." And suddenly there was with the angel a multitude of the heavenly host, praising God and saying,

> "Glory to God in the highest heaven,
> and on earth peace among those whom he favors!"

When the angels had left them and gone into heaven, the shepherds said to one another, "Let us go now to Bethlehem and see this thing that has taken place, which the Lord has made known to us." So they went with haste and found Mary and Joseph, and the child lying in the manger. When they saw this, they made known what had been told them about this

child; and all who heard it were amazed
at what the shepherds told them. But
Mary treasured all these words and pondered them in her heart. The shepherds
returned, glorifying and praising God for
all they had heard and seen, as it had been
told them.

LUKE 2:1–20

The cave in Bethlehem is still warm. Today one group of pilgrims after another
crowds into it. They light their candles, kiss
the star under the altar, listen to the gospel,
and sing hymns in many languages. It is sad
both that Jesus had to turn to the warm earth
and humble animals for welcome, because no
human heart was warm enough to provide room
for him, and that humans today pay their curious tribute even while they desecrate his earth
and abuse his animals for their own selfish ends.

At least we are all impelled to bend our proud
necks to come here. The large door of the basilica was blocked many centuries ago (so that
Muslims could not ride their horses inside), and
each pilgrim must now bow low and edge his or

her way in. Fitting indeed. The wonder of it! Our God—*God himself*—bowed down. He—God—was born in a cave. The displaced, the dispossessed, who live in great numbers in similar surroundings all over the world today, can find some comfort in knowing that God so loves them that he became one of them. An alien government that worshiped its own fabricated gods dominated the Newborn's mother and her husband and dragged them from their home and daily work, from their peaceful life at such a crucial moment in it. But sad to say, even worse tyranny on the part of their own puppet ruler would send them fleeing for their lives into an alien land. Is there anything we suffer that Jesus did not also suffer?

How could the Divine enter more completely and more nakedly into the human experience?

Quickly, the swaddling clothes, those so carefully prepared by Mary, hide his nakedness, protect his vulnerability. Who wants a God so vulnerable, so human, so needy?

He became like us in all things but sin.

Hands through the centuries reach out to him. We need, in our weakness, sin, and misery, a God who is compassionately vulnerable.

Can a God so vulnerable not be compassionate with our weakness? Indeed it is our weakness that he has taken on to be so vulnerable.

He lies there, almost like a life cast out of the warm embracing sanctuary of the womb. The divine is cast upon our earth, clothing himself with all our earthliness.

We sometimes need to be shocked by seeing God in all his humanity—even his sexuality. We are all too prone to leave God out of whole areas of our life. But he wants in. He became— fully, freely, because he wanted it—one with us in our humanness. And every detail of it. He did not sin. But he embraced our sin and carried it with his sinless and totally vulnerable body to the nakedness of the cross. Again, people saw the nakedness of God as he hung there, hiding nothing of his humanity, crucified, in agony, because we in so many ways fail to accept the fullness of our humanity. And all too often live more like animals than integrated humans.

Naked he came forth from the womb. In the womb of Mary he knew the embrace of a love worthy of him. He left the embrace—as painful as was the separation for him and for her—to be here for us.

How can even the most despised of sinners fear to approach a tiny newborn?

He came for us and for our salvation. He wants to be totally available to us, totally accessible. With all the attractive neediness of a tiny one, he lies there inviting our love and care.

Yet there is something about this Newborn that causes our outreaching hands to fold in prayer. For us and for our salvation he is here.

He speaks to us, too, of the sacredness of all life. If all the fullness of the Godhead can be present to us corporally in this littlest bit of humanity, then how can any least bit of humanity not be most sacred? The poor eyes with which we fail to see—to see the divine beauty hidden in every human. How easily are we deceived, blinded by color, shape, what we call deformity, disease. This little Jewish child, one more to be counted in the hated census of the august Romans. This child is our God!

Come, let us adore.

And let our eyes be opened, our vision perfected. Let us see the divine in every child, in the womb or out, in every human. And let us reverence.

Let us reach out, to give the support that is needed, to get the support we need. Human solidarity took on a new dimension when God became one of us. There is nothing of humanity that is not divinized—nothing of the divine that does not now belong to us, to each one of us. Hence the sacredness of all human life—because God did become man—human. He came forth from the womb of a woman—of a human. And presented himself to us as a vulnerable little human with hands and heart and a genitalia that would know the knife of circumcision. Behold, here is our God. If only we can be shocked enough to truly adore.

Our Father…

The Fourth Joyful Mystery

The Presentation

When the time came for their purification according to the law of Moses, they brought him up to Jerusalem to present him to the Lord (as it is written in the law of the Lord, "Every firstborn male shall be designated as holy to the Lord"), and they offered a sacrifice according to what is stated in the law of the Lord, "a pair of turtledoves or two young pigeons." Now there was a man in Jerusalem whose name was Simeon; this man was righteous and devout, looking forward to the consolation of Israel, and the Holy Spirit rested on him. It had been revealed to him by the Holy Spirit that he would not see death before he had seen the Lord's Messiah. Guided by the Spirit, Simeon came into the temple; and when the parents brought in the child Jesus, to do for him what was customary under the law,

Simeon took him in his arms and praised
God, saying,

> "Master, now you are dismissing
>   your servant in peace,
>   according to your word;
> for my eyes have seen your
>   salvation,
>   which you have prepared in the
>   presence of all peoples,
> a light for revelation to the
>   Gentiles
>   and for glory to your people
>   Israel."

And the child's father and mother were
amazed at what was being said about him.
Then Simeon blessed them and said to
his mother Mary, "This child is destined
for the falling and the rising of many in
Israel, and to be a sign that will be opposed so that the inner thoughts of many
will be revealed—and a sword will pierce
your own soul too." There was also a
prophet, Anna the daughter of Phanuel,
of the tribe of Asher. She was of a great
age, having lived with her husband seven
years after her marriage, then as a widow

to the age of eighty-four. She never left the temple but worshiped there with fasting and prayer night and day. At that moment she came, and began to praise God and to speak about the child to all who were looking for the redemption of Jerusalem.

LUKE 2:22–38

The journey from Bethlehem to Jerusalem is not a long one—six or seven miles—though long enough a walk for a young mother who had given birth only forty days earlier and for a young father carrying that most precious of sons. The golden walls of Jerusalem appear soon enough, then the walls of the Temple and the great Golden Gate, closed now almost since the days when the Son of Man last passed through them.

The Temple is quiet today. There are few pilgrims. Strikes and fear of war keep them away. Because no one knows exactly how the vast Temple area was laid out before the destruction, Jews now are not supposed to enter the area, lest they step within what was the Holy of

Holies. Mary and Joseph would have brought the Child through the Court of the Gentiles and the Court of the Women to the entrance of the Court of the Israelites, where Simeon would have met them. That holy old man took the Child into his arms: "Master, now you are dismissing your servant in peace, according to your word..." (Luke 2:29).

Mary holds her Child a bit more tightly. She holds him close to her breast. There is a certain foreboding. Why?

Perhaps it is because this is the temple, the house of his Father. And she is made all too aware of other claims that can be made on her son. *Every firstborn shall be called holy to the Lord.*

Perhaps it is the two little pigeons that are to be offered in sacrifice. There is something fearful about sacrifice: the destruction of life, innocent life, the just for the unjust. Mary is happy that her husband has not disappeared into the Court of the Israelites with the minister who takes their offering to the priests. (This most holy of all God's creatures, this woman is not considered worthy to enter into the inner precincts of this holy place—just because she is a woman.) His warm, strong arm is most comforting.

Perhaps it is Simeon who now approaches them. There is a deep joy in his face, a serenity, a peace. But when she looks into his eyes, Mary sees something else. Looking into those eyes the young mother experiences a great reluctance to place her Little One into his outstretched arms. Men can be so clumsy in handling such fragility.

Yet she cannot refuse.

He does indeed hold her Little One with much gentle loving care. Yet his eyes are not on the Little One. They are on her. The prophetic words pour forth: "Master… my eyes have seen your salvation, which you have prepared in the presence of all peoples, a light for revelation to the Gentiles and for glory to your people Israel" (Luke 2:29–32). And then those words that do exactly what they speak of: "This child is destined for the falling and the rising of many in Israel, and to be a sign that will be opposed—and a sword will pierce your own soul too" (Luke 2:34–35). The sword plunges deep into the soul of the young mother. What should be a most happy moment for this young couple is marred. All Mary's foreboding seems to be realized. This visit to the Temple, to his Father's house, affirms the higher claims upon him. He is to be the savior of his people, as the angel had fore-told. And salvation comes through sacrifice. The drops of blood poured out upon the altar from the little pigeons foretell another outpouring of blood that Mary would rather not envision at this moment—or ever.

Many years later the day would come when Mary would approach her son and he would take it as the occasion to give an important teaching a teaching begun with a question as is the rabbinical way: "Who is my mother?…whoever does the will of my Father in heaven is my…mother" (Matthew 12:48, 50).

Christ has been conceived in each of us at baptism. And we are called to mother the Christ-nature within us.

We bring him to the temple that is within. And we know our own foreboding as we come to the gates of the sanctuary, and reason and imagination, which are usually so much in charge of everything, are asked to let go and we are invited to enter into the deeper, apparently dark regions of the contemplative communion of Christ with his Father. We fear what it might mean: the sacrifice of all that we have come to be identified with as the false self. It is hard to let go. We cherish the Christ within us. But if we do not let go he cannot be about his Father's business—bringing us to full participation in the Christ life. He will be restricted to *our* business.

We have our reluctance, our fear, too, in entrusting this Christ-life of ours to the hands of the priests—the doddering old priests who seem so inept, the careless priests who do not seem to be sensitive to all our concerns, the priests who call to a sacrifice and a mission that seem to be beyond us. Yet without church and sacrament we cannot enter fully into the all-redeeming sacrifice of the Christ whom we are called to be.

And what of that other pair of eyes upon us, the eyes of Anne? Mary's own mother had been an Anne. There was something of motherly tenderness and compassion present in this holy old woman in this hour when the young mother heard the words of dire prophecy already being fulfilled: *and a sword will pierce your own soul too.* His mission, the mission of her Son, is glorious, hope is renewed, but a sword does indeed pierce the all-too-knowing soul of the young mother.

What for all the people, for all of us, is a sign of great joy—the coming of our Savior, the all-saving sacrifice, into the temple of the Father—has its cost. And that cost cut deeply into the soul of this beautiful young mother. A day of purest joy and promise, the coming of the Savior into his temple, the beginning of the work of salvation is not without its birth pains. As long as we are on the journey through this vale of tears, joy and pain are not far apart. This is a joyful mystery, for he has come for us and for our salvation. But it has its pain written deep within for the cost of our salvation is his crucifixion. And we who have been baptized into Christ must share in that pain.

Our Father…

The Fifth Joyful Mystery

The Finding in the Temple

Now every year his parents went to Jerusalem for the festival of the Passover. And when he was twelve years old, they went up as usual for the festival. When the festival was ended and they started to return, the boy Jesus stayed behind in Jerusalem, but his parents did not know it. Assuming that he was in the group of travelers, they went a day's journey. Then they started to look for him among their relatives and friends. When they did not find him, they returned to Jerusalem to search for him. After three days they found him in the temple, sitting among the teachers, listening to them and asking them questions. And all who heard him were amazed at his understanding and his answers. When his parents saw him they were astonished; and his mother said to him, "Child, why have you treated us like this? Look, your father and I have been searching for you in great anxiety." He said to them, "Why were you searching for me? Did you not know that I must be in my Father's house?" But they did not understand what he said to them. Then he went down with them and came to Nazareth, and was obedient to them. His mother treasured all these things in her heart.

And Jesus increased in wisdom and in years, and in divine and human favor.

LUKE 2:41–52

T hings change yet ever remain the same. In the caverns along the wall of the Temple, hundreds of men and boys of all ages are gathered. Some are intent upon their prayer, standing close to the wall or sitting, bowing, and shifting. Others gather in groups, chanting as they sway rhythmically. Some sit in twos or threes, earnestly discussing the Scriptures; at times they even seem to be arguing. How easy it would have been for young Jesus to stay behind for days in a crowd like this. There are many here twelve years of age or younger. Just a few feet from me two young people arrive with their schoolbags, find two chairs and draw them together, take out their books, and become immediately engrossed in discussion. They can be only twelve or thirteen, if that. Another youngster wanders by obviously in search of someone—perhaps his father or a rebbe. The cadences of sound rise and fall.

And Jewish mothers are Jewish mothers. They may not be allowed to enter this precinct of men, but they hover outside in their own area. These are a communal people. The rabbi has his flock. The extended family cares and can be trusted. No one seems to worry about the children who run about; they are in the care of all. No wonder Jesus' staying behind was not noticed until the evening of the first day's journey back.

But why did Jesus stay behind? "Did you not know that I must be in my Father's house?" What is he implying that Mary should have been aware of? He is a man now by Jewish law.. He has his rights and his duties and his responsibilities, yet he is still subject. He acknowledges this and lives it. Sometimes it is not so clear what we owe to God and what we owe to others: parents, superiors, hierarchs, civil authorities, our fellow humans. It was clear to Jesus, and he knew how to coordinate his responsibilities. Others did not understand—even his sinless mother. Later some were threatened by his clarity and even plotted his death. His mother, even in her pain—and free enough to give expression to some annoyance with God—only questioned.

He is still Mary's little boy. He always will be. But a searing school of detachment will assert another reality. In his divine wisdom the Child decided it is time to begin these harsh lessons.

The emotions are high here, many and mixed. Mary's anguished heart knows a great relief. She clings to her child. She presses her face against his. She wants not only to touch him, but to smell him. She would taste him, if she could. The deepest human instincts of a mother are at play here.

Her relief is great, but her anguish, so powerfully present for three days, must have its outlet. "Child, why have you treated us like this? Look, your father and I have been searching for you in great anxiety."

What thoughts possessed the mind of this inward man?

It had been almost twelve years since he accompanied her to this Temple. Together, in ritual offering they acknowledged this child belonged to God. Of all the firstborn he was the Firstborn—the Son of the Most High, the angel had said. This reality remained perhaps more present to Joseph as he reflectively went about his daily life. Though he trained the young hands to the carpenter's tasks, I do not think he ever forgot that this Little One who called him "*abba*" was not in truth his son. This fact in no way lessened his anguish these past few days. The paternity he shared was necessarily mysterious. If anything it demanded of him a love and care beyond that of any mortal fatherhood. In the reunion and in the dialogue that ensued he could only wonder, marvel, experience more profoundly that attitude we call humility.

Mary, as true mother, and perhaps even more enlightened than Joseph in regard to the real nature of her son, with a profound joy and deep realization had brought their son to his Father, fully acknowledging that this firstborn is his Firstborn. But as the weeks and months and years went by and she enjoyed all the intimacies and services of a mother toward her little one, it was very easy to forget that there was another dimension to this son of hers. He was so like every other little boy—*like us in all things but sin*. Yes, at the presentation Mary had wholeheartedly given her son to his Father. Yet, she was not prepared for the Father to so suddenly take him, for her Twelve-Year-Old to suddenly leave the long-accepted pattern and be about his Father's business, remaining in his Father's house.

How often in moments of fervor have we offered ourselves completely to God? We are all his—to do with us whatever he wants. And then one day— it usually seems quite sudden—he claims what has been offered to him. He steps into our lives with some new claim, perhaps some cross, a new vocation or a shift in the ongoing pattern of our life. Perhaps he seems to have walked out of our lives; he is no longer with us—all too docile to our wills. "Lord, why have you done this to me?"

His answer to us is as it was to Mary: "Did you not know I must be about my Father's business?"—that business of helping us become selfless, self-giving saints.

We had best be careful what we say to the Lord in our moments of fervor. He takes us seriously. Fortunately for us, grace moves us to moments of loving folly. We are ready to give all. We offer all. Know well: He will take all. That is what he wants. He'll be satisfied with nothing less. Because he wants to wholly transform us to divine children beatifically happy, filled to overflowing with the divine joy.

If as we pray our beads he seems to be lost to us, be comforted. Seek him as Mary and Joseph, assured that with them we will find him and find that he is about his Father's loving business of making us his saints, his holy, wholly happy ones.

Our Father…

The Five
Mysteries
of Light

Moving on from the infancy and the hidden life in Nazareth to the public life of Jesus, our contemplation brings us to those mysteries that may be called in a special way "mysteries of light." Certainly the whole mystery of Christ is a mystery of light. He is the "light of the world" (John 8:12). Yet this truth emerges in a special way during the years of his public life, when he proclaims the Gospel of the Kingdom. In proposing to the Christian community five significant moments — "luminous" mysteries—during this phase of Christ's life, I think that the following can be fittingly singled out: (1) his Baptism in the Jordan, (2) his self-manifestation at the wedding of Cana, (3) his proclamation of the Kingdom of God, with his call to conversion, (4) his Transfiguration, and finally, (5) his institution of the Eucharist, as the sacramental expression of the Paschal Mystery.

Each of these mysteries is a revelation of the Kingdom now present in the very person of Jesus.

"APOSTOLIC LETTER OF POPE JOHN PAUL II
ON THE MOST HOLY ROSARY:
ROSARIUM VIRGINIS MARIAE," 21

The First Mystery of Light
The Baptism in the Jordan

Then Jesus came from Galilee to John at
the Jordan, to be baptized by him. John
would have prevented him, saying, "I
need to be baptized by you, and do you
come to me?" But Jesus answered him,
"Let it be so now; for it is proper for us in
this way to fulfill all righteousness." Then
he consented. And when Jesus had been
baptized, just as he came up from the
water, suddenly the heavens were opened
to him and he saw the Spirit of God de-
scending like a dove and alighting on
him. And a voice from heaven said, "This
is my Son, the Beloved, with whom I am
well pleased."

MATTHEW 3:13–17

The descent from the Holy City is steep enough, pervaded by the dry barren atmosphere of the Desert of Judea. The Jordan River valley is said to be the deepest in the world. As the river pours forth, fresh and lively and full of fish, from the lake so dear to Jesus, the Sea of Galilee, it is already seven hundred feet below sea level. It pursues its course through what is initially a lush valley, winding this way and that, taking some 220 miles to reach its point of entry into the Dead Sea, only 70 miles south, as the crow flies. And all the time it descends more and more, 1,290 feet below sea level when it enters the deadly sea that quickly kills any fish that have survived the journey south. A good distance before it reaches this scene of desolation, the river valley begins to lose its verdure and take on some of the features of its terminus.

It is probably in one of the eddies not far from the main river crossing below Jericho, that the strange figure who comes out of the desert, the prophet, John the Baptizer, takes up his position. Here the crowds easily gather. Here he more easily stands in the shallows and his responsive penitents safely approach him without fear of the river current. One might wonder if this man had spent his days in the desert howling against the wind, for his voice is robust and clear. His garb bespeaks the desert: a hide he inherited from some camel that perished in the wilderness and a leather belt. He is said to have survived on locusts and wild honey, products of his chosen habitat. Whatever nourished him, he now comes forth lean and strong, with a certain fierceness about him. But certainly not unreasonable in the face of goodwill: "Whoever has two coats must share with anyone who has none; and whoever has food must do likewise…. Collect no more than the amount prescribed for you…. Do not extort money from anyone by threats or false accusation, and be satisfied with your wages" (Luke 3:11, 13–14).

The crowds come and the crowds go: the true seekers, like the two young men from the shores of the Sea of Galilee; the curious and restless; and the officious challengers. They stand on the shore and watch and listen, perhaps seeking a bit of shade among the straggling growth there. And in a moment of grace many step forward into the waters and receive John's baptism of repentance. But John makes no bones about it. His is but a preparation for what is to come: "I baptize you in water for repentance, but the one who is more powerful than I is coming after me; I am not worthy to carry his sandals. He will baptize you with the Holy Spirit and fire" (Matthew 3:11).

Then the day comes. There steps out of the crowd on the shore a familiar figure. We do not know how often these cousins had been together. In a sense, John had known his cousin Jesus even before he was born. For he was still in the womb when Jesus, himself in the womb, visited him and sanctified him. Undoubtedly, in the course of the annual pilgrimages to the Holy City, Joseph and his family would have visited with the nearby relatives. Just when the young John went forth to the desert, we do not know. He must have been made aware of his mission early on. His father would have repeated for him the message of the angel:

> Your wife Elizabeth will bear you a son, and you will name him John. You will have joy and gladness, and many will rejoice at his birth, for he will be great in the sight of the Lord. He must never drink wine or strong drink; even before his birth he will be filled with the Holy Spirit. He will turn many of the people of Israel to

the Lord their God. With the spirit and power of Elijah he will go before him, to turn the hearts of parents to their children, and the disobedient to the wisdom of the righteous, to make ready a people prepared for the Lord (Luke 1:13–17).

Indeed, at John's circumcision, his chastened father proclaimed before all:

And you, child, will be called the
     prophet of the Most High;
  for you will go before the Lord to
     prepare his ways,
to give knowledge of salvation to
     his people
  by the forgiveness of their sins.
By the tender mercy of our God,
  the dawn from on high will
     break upon us,
to give light to those who sit in
     darkness and in the
     shadow of death,
  to guide our feet into the way of peace.

LUKE 1:76–79

There is no hesitation now. John recognizes his cousin. And he knows the right order of things. It is for him to be baptized by this cousin; "I need to be baptized by you…." But Jesus knows the whole score. Jesus knows how "salvation through the forgiveness of sins" is to come about. It is time for him to begin his saving mission, which can lead only to Calvary "to fulfill all righteousness." After Jesus' final preparation of the sojourn in the desert, John will point him out: "Behold, there is the Lamb of God, who takes away the sin of the world." Jesus is taking upon himself, as a sacrificial lamb, the sin of us all. An act of repentance is fitting.

Yet he who will say to us. "Learn of me for I am meek and humble of heart" will not imperiously demand that his cousin fall into line with his mission. There was only a gentle "permit it now." And John humbly allows for it. To what a moment their collaborative humility opens the way! It is the moment of a mystery of light.

As Jesus comes up out of the water, the very skies are rent open. John has his promised theophany: "The one who sent me to baptize with water told me: 'On whomever you see the Spirit come down and remain, he is the one who will baptize with Holy Spirit.'" "John sees the

Spirit of God coming down as a dove, coming upon him." And more: "A voice out of the heavens saying, "This is my Son, the Beloved, in whom I am well pleased." It is a moment of light indeed, a moment of ultimate revelation. To human ears is imparted the mystery hidden from all ages: God is Triune. Not only does God have a Son, a perfect and total expression of God-self, but the communion of Love between the Father and Son is the fullness of God, their Holy Spirit. And this young man, this young carpenter from Nazareth who is shortly to begin his career as a rabbi, is the Son, the term of the Love.

How much John understands in this moment is not clear to us. (Indeed, how much do we understand in the face of this awesome mystery of Life and Love?) In a way his mission is complete. Yet he will go on and keep trying to turn "the disobedient to the understanding of the righteous, to prepare a people fit for the Lord" even at the cost of his head.

For Jesus, the "hidden life" is over. He will still go apart at times to prepare himself with prayer. In fact, the Gospel of Saint Mark tells us, at this very moment when he is to embark upon his public ministry, "the Spirit drove him out into the desert." But from now on his face is set toward Jerusalem. He will seek always to do the things that will please the Father. He belongs to the people, the lost sheep of the house of Israel, whom he comes to save. He belongs to us all "because of the tender mercy of our God…to shine on those who sit in darkness and death's shadow, to guide our feet into the path of peace."

The heavens open not only for Jesus but also for us. By his own baptism Jesus gives us the wonderful sacrament of baptism. In time he will send forth his disciples to bring this gift to all peoples. For each of us, the heavens will open, Holy Spirit will come down upon us. Christ's Spirit will become our Spirit. We will be baptized into Christ, into a oneness with him that is beyond anything we can comprehend. He himself will liken it to the oneness he has with the Father, an absolute oneness of being. As we come up out of the waters of baptism, the Father says of each one of us: This is my child, my beloved.

Our Father…

The Second Mystery of Light

The Manifestation
of Jesus at Cana

On the third day there was a wedding in Cana of Galilee, and the mother of Jesus was there. Jesus and his disciples had also been invited to the wedding. When the wine gave out, the mother of Jesus said to him, "They have no wine." And Jesus said to her, "Woman, what concern is that to you and to me? My hour has not yet come." His mother said to the servants, "Do whatever he tells you." Now standing there were six stone water jars for the Jewish rites of purification, each holding twenty or thirty gallons. Jesus said to them, "Fill the jars with water." And they filled them up to the brim. He said to them, "Now draw some out, and take it to the chief steward." So they took it. When the steward tasted the water that had become wine, and did not know where it came from (though the servants who had drawn the water knew), the steward called the bridegroom and said to him, "Everyone serves the good wine first, and then the inferior wine after the guests have become drunk. But you have kept the good wine until now." Jesus did this, the first of his signs, in Cana of Galilee, and revealed his glory; and his disciples believed in him.

JOHN 2:1–11

E ven today as one travels north along the road, Cana does not stand out as much more than a village of no great consequence. The twin-towered church, built by the Franciscans early in the last century, is its mark of distinction and the primary goal of the many visitors or pilgrims who stop here. Back in Jesus' time it was the little synagogue with its resident rabbi that gathered the cluster of humble homes and shops. Excavations give evidence that this synagogue became in the first century the gathering place of Jewish

Christians while a larger synagogue was built near the edge of town. And there is the village fountain. There is nothing to say that it is not the very same fountain from which the waiters drew the water that Jesus changed into wine. One might be a bit more skeptical about the authenticity of the large pots on display. They could hardly have withstood twenty centuries of tumultuous history. There is another church in town, too, said to mark the site of the home of Nathaniel, son of Tolomeus, the young disciple in whom Jesus said there is no guile.

This may be why Jesus is in town. He has just begun gathering disciples. His public commission at his baptism and his preparation in the desert were complete. Now he will go back to his own town, Nazareth, and begin preaching the good news, fulfilling the prophecy of the great Isaiah. But today is a very special day in Cana, a village just about seven miles north of Nazareth. It is a wedding day, the highpoint in the life of any Jew.

The whole town will turn out. Friends and relatives will be there from near and far. Jesus may be known there, the carpenter from nearby Nazareth coming up for one job or another. His mother certainly is; in fact she may be a relative of the family. Mary is there and proud and happy to see her son there with the fine men who seem to be surrounding him with a certain devotion.

The festivities are going full swing. The groom has arrived with his companions to claim his bride. The marriage contract was formally signed. The couple expressed their commitment to each other and received the rabbinical blessing. And now singing and dancing fills the house and all the open space around it. And the wine flows freely.

It is perhaps something innate to motherhood, but Mary is one of the first to notice the concern among the waiters gathered around the wineskins. Their pitchers are emptying fast and there is no more wine in the skins. If the wine ever runs out…. The crowd might turn sullen. In any case there would be great embarrassment for the family and the village. The gossip would begin which would never end as long as the couple lived. At every family mishap it would be said: Remember, the wine ran out at their wedding feast. The joyous procession to the groom's house as he takes his bride home, completing the festivities, will not be so joyous. In fact it will be a disaster.

Mary knows who can remedy the situation, though perhaps she has no idea just how he will do it. She approaches her beautiful son and whispers in his ear: They have no wine.

Jesus' recorded response is one of those passages in the Sacred Text that keeps us humble. Just what precisely did he say and what did it mean? The translations of the Greek text are many and variant. Is it an affirmation that since his public commissioning from heaven at the Jordan he is no longer the submissive child of Nazareth? Or is he trying to say that as far as he is concerned things are not all yet in place for him to begin his public ministry? Am I being too anthropomorphic to suggest that maybe Jesus is squirming a bit at the thought that it will be recorded that his first sign is a miracle to turn out more booze for the boys after they have drunk the house dry? (Certainly the disciples he brought along were not among the expected guests and probably did more than their share to help create the shortage!)

In any case, Mother will not be put off. Mary's words to the waiters, the Virgin Mother's last recorded words, are words we can all take to heart: Do whatever he tells you.

Jesus' eyes sweep the area. He could miraculously refill the empty skins that hang along the wall. Or fill those big jugs that stand by the entrance. They had been filled with water for the guests to perform the required ablutions before the meal. But in this first sign as in all others Jesus wants us to have our part. Plain ordinary everyday things and human activity will almost always be part of the story. The concerned waiters are told to fill the large pots to the brim. And to the extent that they obey—and they do, all the way—they will have an abundance of the best of wines.

There is some wonderment at the quality of the late wine, especially on the part of the master of the feast, but the celebration goes on without a hitch. The waiters say little, most would probably have said they had sipped too much of the wine themselves. Only Jesus' devoted band are fully aware of this first sign that Jesus works. Their devotion to the rabbi takes another leap: they believe in him, not only because of the sign but also because of the example of the woman, his mother, who obviously has no doubt as to his love and his care, his power and his willingness to respond, even in the face of an initial enigmatic response. She who mothered him is now mothering his disciples in faith.

So many things Jesus is teaching us here. Yes, there is a place in life for joy and celebration. Yes, marriage is a supreme moment in life. In time it will become clear that it is a sacrament of his own loving union with us, his people, his church. Yes, a heavenly Father, so filled with compassionate love and care, provides for us the tenderness of a loving and watchful mother who will bring all our needs to a Son who cannot deny her anything. Yes, his works are signs of faith: Believe because of what I do. Yes, God, so completely human, is in our midst in joy as well as sorrow. Nothing human (even a cup of wine— or two or three) is foreign to him.

Our Father…

The Third Mystery of Light

The Proclamation
~~of the Kingdom~~

Now after John was arrested, Jesus came to Galilee, proclaiming the good news of God, and saying, "The time is fulfilled, and the kingdom of God has come near; repent, and believe in the good news."

MARK 1:14–15

Then some people came, bringing to him a paralyzed man, carried by four of them. And when they could not bring him to Jesus because of the crowd, they removed the roof above him; and after having dug through it, they let down the mat on which the paralytic lay. When Jesus saw their faith, he said to the paralytic, "Son, your sins are forgiven." Now some of the scribes were sitting there, questioning in their hearts, "Why does this fellow speak in this way? It is blasphemy! Who can forgive sins but God alone?" At once Jesus perceived in his spirit that they were discussing these questions among themselves; and he said to them, "Why do you raise such questions in your hearts? Which is easier, to say to the paralytic, 'Your sins are forgiven,' or to say, 'Stand up and take your mat and walk'? But so that you may know that the Son of Man has authority on earth to forgive sins"— he said to the paralytic—"I say to you, stand up, take your mat and go to your home." And he stood up, and immediately took the mat and went out before all of them; so that they were all amazed and glorified God, saying, "We have never seen anything like this!"

MARK 2:3–12

One of the Pharisees asked Jesus to eat with him, and he went into the Pharisee's house and took his place at the table. And a woman in the city, who was a sinner, having learned that he was eating in the Pharisee's house, brought an alabaster jar of ointment. She stood behind him at his feet, weeping, and began to bathe his feet with her tears and to dry them with her hair. Then she continued kissing his feet and anointing them with the ointment. Now when the Pharisee who had invited him saw it, he said to himself, "If this man were a prophet, he would have known who and what kind of woman this is who is touching him—that she is a sinner." Jesus spoke up and said to him, "Simon, I have something to say to you." "Teacher," he replied, "Speak." "A certain creditor had two debtors; one owed five hundred denarii, and the other fifty. When they could not pay, he canceled the debts for both of them. Now which of them will love him more?" Simon answered, "I suppose the one for whom he canceled the greater debt." And Jesus said to him, "You have judged rightly." Then turning toward the woman, he said to Simon, "Do you see this woman? I entered your house; you gave me no water for my feet, but she has bathed my feet with her tears and dried them with her hair. You gave me no kiss, but from the time I came in she has not stopped kissing my feet. You did not anoint my head with oil, but she has anointed my feet with ointment. Therefore, I tell you, her sins, which were many, have been forgiven; hence she has shown great love. But the one to whom little is forgiven, loves little." Then he said to her, "Your sins are forgiven." But those who were at the table with him began to say among themselves, "Who is this who even forgives sins?" And he said to the woman, "Your faith has saved you; go in peace."

LUKE 7:36–50

When it was evening on that day, the first day of the week, and the doors of the house where the disciples had met were locked for fear of the Jews, Jesus came and stood among them and said, "Peace be with you." After he said this, he showed them his hands and his side. Then the disciples rejoiced when they saw the Lord. Jesus said to them again, "Peace be with you. As the Father has sent me, so I send you." When he had said this, he breathed on them and said to them, "Receive the Holy Spirit. If you forgive the sins of any,

they are forgiven them; if you retain the
sins of any, they are retained."

JOHN 20:19–23

Among this very communal people, the
family of the People of God, the sons
and daughters of Abraham, the home was a
very communal place. The entry from the road
leads immediately into a large open area. The
cooking might be done off in a corner, the
supplies nearby and a place for the wash-up.
There are large pots of water by the entrance
reserved for the ritual washings. Among the
more affluent there might be in the center a
large, low table with divans arranged around
it where the men could lounge while they ate,
drank, and discussed anything that could be
discussed and more. Among the poorer, some
floor covering, mats, or the swept earth had
to suffice. Women knew their place, back in
the service areas except when they were to
come forward to serve.

Any man might well step through the usually wide-open door. And he would know that
he would be welcome to join in whatever was

going on—the law of hospitality. When a special guest arrived or there was a celebration or a feast, the area might become crowded indeed.

When the Rabbi, the Master, came to town, the home into which he chose to enter quickly became the focal point of all activity. Men would crowd in to see and hear him; women, to help with the service.

It wasn't that what this Rabbi was saying was all that new. It was similar to what the Baptizer had preached in his own way; what prophets through the centuries had proclaimed as the message from on high. And in a sense it was not all that appealing: "The Kingdom of God has drawn near; repent and believe…." But it was a message that spoke to the heart, to the deepest place within, of anyone who had ears to hear. The way the Master said it, the ramifications he drew out from it, the signs and wonders with which he confirmed it—these attracted maximum attention.

This third Mystery of Light invites us to range widely in the public ministry of Christ. All was a "proclamation of the Kingdom of God." a "call to conversion." The pope in his very concise presentation of the mystery points to two particular instances exemplifying Christ's "ministry of mercy." They seem to reach for a certain universality: The subject of one is a man, of the other, a woman. In the one case, the event seems to take place in a common home and the folks crowd in, filling every space. In the other, we are in the home of the wealthy and the eager, listening crowd respectfully keeps its distance. In the first case, the recipient of mercy arrives there only with the help of his faithful friends. In the other, the penitent has to courageously make her own way through, experiencing the repulsion of those about. The one says not a word, seems to be almost totally passive, carried by his friends. The other is intensely active, letting tears and kisses express what words could never quite manage. In the one case faith is proclaimed, power is affirmed, and sin is linked with its consequences. In the other, it is faith, alive in great love, and its expressions that are set before us.

The Gospel of Mark seems to want to bring out the communal dimension of Jesus' "ministry of mercy." The first healing it recounts takes place in a gathering of the people in the synagogue. Then Peter brings Jesus to his house and in so doing he brings healing first to his family and then to all who come there. The shift from synagogue to Peter's is significant (in the literal sense) for us. But in the next miracle, the cure of the leper, Jesus acknowledges the authority of the priest. As the second chapter of the Gospel opens, we have this instance that the pope points to: crowds are gathered to Jesus, a new people is forming. The companions—they may well have been his companions in sin, but it is sure they are loving and caring companions— are intent upon bringing their sinful and afflicted friend to the Master. They will not be put off. In their persistence and ingenuity they will literally raise the roof to place him right before the Lord. I wonder if Jesus smiles as the mat comes down in front of him. In any case, a word, a healing ministry, takes away sin and the effects of sin.

There is something shocking in both of these instances that the pope has chosen. The Master's bald affirmation that he can forgive sin....A prostitute caressing, kissing, massaging with hand and oil and the very hair of her head— such intimacy and in public…. The ministry of mercy is shocking. It throws out all our sense of proportion, justice, and propriety. It bespeaks a love that is beyond our experience, even our conception. It is a God become a servant; even more: a beggar, ready to do anything, to allow anything for our love.

Whether we identify more readily with the man lying helpless on his mat, totally dependent on his friends, or the bold and forthright woman who confronts her shame with an ardent, driving love, we want to get in touch with the grace of conversion in them each. And in all the others who confidently approach the Lord as he goes about proclaiming the Kingdom of love and mercy. Here is a ministry of mercy, one that is not to end even with the supreme act of mercy and love we witness on Calvary. For he will return. He will rise. He will abide in a sacramental ministry.

This is the very heart and center of the Revelation. All else is to make it possible and to help us believe it is possible and is. This ministry of mercy cannot be confined to the time of the public ministry. It must reach beyond, indeed, to the end of time. And so the pope points beyond, inviting us to the upper room on the day of the Resurrection.

For Jesus disciples there is a sort of love-hate relationship with the room now. It is a fairly safe place for them to meet—or to tell the truth, hide. Few would know where they are and their genial host will protect them as best he can. But there are the memories of Thursday night and after. He said they would all betray him, and they did. John, the young one, the Master's beloved, did return and stick to the end. Peter, who had so miserably failed, now hangs close to this lad. There is a lingering presence of Judas, traitor and suicide. Even before they are a formally constituted church the church has to cope with these deep wounds. His beautiful, heartfelt words hang in the air—what do they mean now?

They are grateful that a Sabbath has intervened. It was a quiet day with few stirring abroad. One can stay at home, eat what had been prepared beforehand, rest and pray. Largely in silence they passed the day.

And now the first day of the week is upon them. And what a chaotic day it has been. Women who went to anoint the body came back with tales of angles and an empty tomb. Peter and John had also rushed out and saw only an empty tomb. Or did they see more in the arrangement of the cloths? Then the Magdalene burst in upon them, saying she saw him. She, who stayed at the cross until the end, had every right to be distraught. But there was something about her obvious, deep joy. Then a bemused Peter came back: he too had seen. What are they to make of all this? By the time the two who had headed out to Emmaus, totally discouraged—"We had hoped"—burst into the room, the room is filled with chaotic joy, wonderment, questioning, efforts to reassure one another, as they recount again and again the stories of Peter and John, Mary and the other women.

Then suddenly, there he is. There he is, standing in their midst. No door opened. No window. But he is there. Before the question can arise from their stunned minds, their churning hearts, in totally unghostlike fashion he asks for something to eat, takes a bite of fish, chews it, and swallows. A perfectly normal human. But not quite.

It is the Lord. His greeting of peace gradually brings his peace into their hearts. What was too good to be true, is true. There he is, with gapping yet lustrous wounds in his hands and feet and his exposed side. It is the Master, the Master who had been crucified.

After such an ordeal, after the shame of betrayal and flight, he gives their troubled minds and hearts peace. And he sends them forth as ministers of that peace, the peace that comes through reconciliation and the forgiveness of sins: "Peace to you. As the Father has sent me, I also send you." Out of the eternal embrace of Divine Love, Jesus, the Son, breathes forth the Spirit of Love and empowers these men to bring the peace of divine reconciliation to others: "Receive Holy Spirit. Whose sins you forgive, they have been forgiven them; whose sins you retain, they have been retained." "Who can forgive sins except God?" And those to whom Divine Mercy imparts such a share in his ministry of mercy. This ministry of mercy is available to each one of us in the sacrament of reconciliation.

Our Father…

The Fourth Mystery of Light
The Transfiguration

Now about eight days after these sayings Jesus took with him Peter and John and James, and went up on the mountain to pray. And while he was praying, the appearance of his face changed, and his clothes became dazzling white. Suddenly they saw two men, Moses and Elijah, talking to him. They appeared in glory and were speaking of his departure, which he was about to accomplish at Jerusalem. Now Peter and his companions were weighed down with sleep; but since they had stayed awake, they saw his glory and the two men who stood with him. Just as they were leaving him, Peter said to Jesus, "Master, it is good for us to be here; let us make three dwellings, one for you, one for Moses, and one for Elijah"—not knowing what he said. While he was saying this, a cloud came and overshadowed them; and they were terrified as they entered the cloud. Then from the cloud came a voice that said, "This is my Son, my Chosen; listen to him!"

LUKE 9:28–35

You can see it from almost any place in eastern Galilee. It is said to be a perfect mountain, it seems so perfectly rounded and smooth. It is only as we approach it we see how very steep it is. Even with the long zigzag road it is a challenging and exhausting climb, too steep for the tourist buses. Only true pilgrims make it to the top of Tabor. It is an immense relief when the medieval stone arch comes into sight. From there it is a straight, tree-lined—and therefore shaded—way right up to the Syrian-style basilica on the summit. The basilica is fairly new, less than a century old. Medieval ruins of Saracen origin can be found to the right and more ancient Christian ruins underneath the crypt. A large Franciscan hospice stands to the right of the basilica while down in the olive groves to the left is a small Orthodox monastery, an oasis of peace. But really we do not need any of these. Tabor is its own sanctuary. As we pray the morning prayer we watch the sun rise out of the Sea of Galilee, which is not far from the base of the mountain. In the evening we retreat to behind the great basilica to watch the sun complete its course and sink into the Mediterranean as we chant our vesper prayer.

It is said that the first atom bomb was exploded over Japan, with all its deadly intent, on the feast of the Transfiguration in mockery of the Light of Tabor. Whatever might have been the comparative physical brightness of the two events, it is certain that the transforming effect of the Light of Tabor was something of a wholly other order. And that transforming enlightenment and grace remains atop Tabor. The seeking pilgrim does not need the great mosaic in the apse of the basilica to experience the glorified Christ on Tabor's summit. He is there and the transforming experience remains even as one comes down from the mountain. After Tabor we see only Christ in every man, woman, and child.

While none of us can ever comprehend the fullness and depth of Jesus' love for us personally and individually, it nonetheless remains that

Jesus does have his favorites. Even among the chosen Twelve there are favorites. It is Peter, the one he chose to be the leader, and the two brothers, James, who is to be the first bishop of Jerusalem, and John, the Beloved, the disciple whom Jesus loves, who are invited to ascend Tabor with him. There was no zigzag road then. Only a rugged footpath. It is a long, hard, hot climb. And they have no idea where he is leading them: will it be all the way to the top? But they follow. Even as we must follow, all the way, if we want to truly "find" Jesus.

The opening scene of the event brings two other participants: Moses, the Lawgiver, and Elijah, the great Prophet. The Jews when they speak of the inspired Scriptures often speak of them as "the Law and the Prophets." It is these two in converse with Jesus, probably drawing out sentences from the Scriptures, who lead the three chosen ones into an initial revelation of what is to take place at Jerusalem. The three are to live through the whole horror of it, in fact one of them would be the sole of the Twelve who will remain steadfast right to the end.

If we would see Jesus, understand what he suffered, come to know its promise, we too must turn to "the Law and the Prophets," to the inspired Scriptures—now aided by those of the New Testament. Our path to contemplation begins in *lectio*, in letting the inspired Word of God enter us, shape us, and call us forward in faith and hope.

The three are elated by this wondrous experience. The exuberant Peter, ever wanting to take charge and do something, has his plan: Lord, let us build here three booths (those little huts, open to the sky, built by the Jews for the week of Succoth). When we have an experience of God, we so much want to capture it, hang on to it, confine it within something our mind can grasp and hold. But that is not possible. Any concept, image or feeling that comes from us is far too confining. It would reduce the experience to mere human dimensions. The Divine experience takes us beyond all that. The evangelist Luke tells us Peter speaks, this time as in others, "not knowing what he was saying."

The Lord takes care of that. The brightness of the transfigured Christ is already beyond anything that human words can describe. The sacred writers scramble for images. If they lived in our times they might well have used the image of the hydrogen bomb or preferably some of the images coming to us from the Hubble telescope. But more is yet to come. It is the Cloud that led the Chosen People out of Egypt, the Cloud that illumined Sinai, that filled the Temple.

I like the traditional icon of the Transfiguration. Jesus stands on the pinnacle of the steep mountain, surrounded by halos of all different colors, Moses and Elijah on either side of him. And the three disciples lay sprawled out in different directions, sandals flying! Human words, thoughts, images, plans, are all gone to the winds. The experience of the moment is all. And a message reverberates within them: "This is my Chosen Son, listen to him." This is the essential message of Tabor, this Mystery of Light: this man, this humble carpenter turned rabbi, from the despicable town of Nazareth, is in fact the very Son of the Most High, the Son of the all-holy and glorious God of heaven and earth. He is the Light, the lightsome Cloud who led the Chosen People out of bondage and will now lead them into the heavenly kingdom: "Listen to him."

As soon as it begins it is all over—or so it seems, for it is not a moment in time but in eternity, in the timeless time of God. At a gentle touch on the shoulder, the awed disciples dare to look up, and they see only Jesus. They see only Jesus, their beloved rabbi. They see only Jesus when they live the faith of the mountain, in every man, woman, and child.

They were silent and at that time reported to no one what they had seen. There is a time and a place for sharing. The Son of Man is now risen. Unfortunately he is not yet risen in every heart. What I have "seen" on the mountain can only be shared by those who have ears to hear, hearts open to hear, the incredibly wondrous truth that God, the glorious God of heaven and earth, did become one with us in our humanity; the faith that can believe and give birth to a hope that can look to the joy of the Resurrection and our own transfiguration through the coming of the Spirit even through the dereliction of Calvary.

Open to the awesome Light of Tabor, we pray:

Our Father…

The Fifth Mystery of Light

The Institution
of the Eucharist

Now before the festival of the Passover, Jesus knew that his hour had come to depart from this world and go to the Father. Having loved his own who were in the world, he loved them to the end.

JOHN 13:1

On the first day of Unleavened Bread, when the Passover lamb is sacrificed, his disciples said to him, "Where do you want us to go and make the preparations for you to eat the Passover?" So he sent two of his disciples, saying to them, "Go into the city, and a man carrying a jar of water will meet you; follow him, and wherever he enters, say to the owner of the house, 'The Teacher asks, Where is my guest room where I may eat the Passover with my disciples?" He will show you a large room upstairs, furnished and ready. Make preparations for us there." So the disciples set out and went to the city, and found everything as he had told them; and they prepared the Passover meal.

When it was evening, he came with the twelve. And when they had taken their places and were eating, Jesus said, "Truly I tell you, one of you will betray me, one who is eating with me." They began to be distressed and to say to him one after another, "Surely, not I?" He said to them, "It is one of the twelve, one who is dipping bread into the bowl with me. For the Son of Man goes as it is written of him, but woe to that one by whom the Son of Man is betrayed! It would have been better for that one not to have been born."

While they were eating, he took a loaf of bread, and after blessing it he broke it, gave it to them, and said, "Take; this is my body." Then he took a cup, and after giving thanks he gave it to them, and all of them drank from it. He said to them, "This is my blood of the covenant, which

is poured out for many. Truly I tell you, I
will never again drink of the fruit of the
vine until that day when I drink it new
in the kingdom of God."

When they had sung the hymn, they
went out to the Mount of Olives.

MARK 14:12–26

*Parallel texts: Matthew 26:17–30; Luke 22:7–20;
1 Corinthians 11:23–26*

The "upper room" they point out today
in Jerusalem is indeed a disappointing
experience. It is hardly more than a big rect-
angular hall, much too big for the supper room,
adorned with some poor gothic features, whose
layout invites all sorts of speculation as to their
original intent. This upper room is a level above
the surrounding streets but undoubtedly far
above the original upper room if it is in truth
located at this site.

Even when the room empties of noisy tour-
ists or pilgrim groups it is difficult to sense the
sacred. It seems so big, empty, and barren. But
then was there anything very special about the

room Jesus sent his disciples to prepare? It was in all probability not much different from many other upper rooms in Jerusalem that were available for the more affluent pilgrim to hire for the celebration of the Passover meal. The disciples had undoubtedly celebrated the meal with their Master in previous years. His particular directions to this room might have seemed a bit unusual but by this time they were used to things being a bit unusual. In any case the meal preparation was quite standard. The lamb was purchased and ritually slain by a Levite at the Temple. Now it roasts on the spit. The table bears the usual elements: the bitter herbs, the unleavened bread, flasks of wine…. All is ready in good time. All is as in the past. Except there hangs in the air a heaviness, a certain sense of foreboding. Rumors are flowing. People are edgy. And expectant after last Sunday's demonstration.

The Master arrives with the rest of the band. The door is closed. They find their places about the low table. Then suddenly the Master rises, lays aside his outer garment, girds himself with a towel, takes up a pitcher and basin, and begins to wash their feet. This is the first of the unsettling events of this evening. He speaks with a depth, with a solemnity, words they can hardly understand, the opening of a heart and more. He foretells a betrayal. Indeed, betrayal on the part of them all. He sends Judas out.

All of this is woven into the age-old ritual. The story of liberation is heard again. The psalms are prayed. The cups are held up in benediction. The bread is broken and a portion is "hidden," the *aphikomon*. The bitter herbs, the lamb are eaten.

As the long meal draws towards its conclusion, the sacredness of the moment possesses the room and all in it more and more. Jesus draws out the hidden portion of unleavened bread. He holds it up before them all and says: "Take, this is my body." With wonder more than comprehension, the bread is broken and passed along among them. As they eat it they know a new communion with the Master. Could any more intimate sign of assimilation be given than this?

The silence hangs heavy but peaceful. It is time for the fourth and final cup, the cup of thanksgiving. But the flask is not passed to fill their cups. Only his cup is filled, filled to the brim. He holds it up and says: "This is my blood of the covenant, being shed for many." No, they will not each drink from his own cup as they had always done in the past. This time they will drink of the one cup, his cup, the cup of his blood. The one whom the Baptizer had pointed out to the first of them as the Lamb of God is to be sacrificed. His blood is to be poured out, a sin offering for them and for all of us.

Tonight is a night of intimacy. The whole structure of the Church, and the world mission it is built on, finds its heart in the intimacy of the Eucharist. It is openness to Christ our Savior ("If I do not wash you, you will have no part in me.") and Communion in body and blood that empowers the Church that we are. This sharing of body, more intimate than any sex, is shocking. "This is my body—eat." How can the Twelve possibly comprehend what is going on? The way we do. By the illumination of the Spirit who enables us to hear, understand, and accept the Word of Christ. Our temptation is to fall back on metaphor: "This is a symbol of my body." But under the sure guidance of the Spirit we know this is body and blood, wrapped in sacramental veils. The completely human heart of the God-man so wants the greatest possible union with us that he calls upon the fullness of his divine power to make the incredible real. Is it any surprise that the great mystical saints assure us that the mystical marriage is always celebrated in the reception of the Eucharist. If we would but open ourselves to it, every time we are privileged to participate in the Eucharist we would know the ecstasy of consummate union with God.

But we don't. Either because of our limited comprehension or our limited time that does not allow our comprehension in faith to rise and blossom, we receive the body and blood with varying degrees of piety but not the surrender to love that lets it work its wonder in us. This is undoubtedly why the Holy Father invites us to give a decade of our contemplative reflection to this sublime mystery of Communion. This is the last of the Mysteries of Light because nothing reveals to us more fully or surely the Divine Lover for whom he made us, how he longs for us, to enjoy us, to be one with us.

The body and the blood in their sacramental separation here repeat his words: "Greater love than this no one has than that one lay down life for a friend." But it goes beyond this. It is a communion sacrifice. The body and blood are food indeed; a sacrifice of being that nourishes the beloved. The whole of the divine humanity, given for us, is given to us. His body enters my body; his blood warms my blood, engendering now a life that is eternal. It is indeed a consummation of love.

They sing their concluding hymn as they set out. They make their way to Olivet for a time of prayer, reflection, and thanksgiving. Poor tired ones, they all soon fell asleep—all except the Master.

Our Father…

The Five
Sorrowful
Mysteries

The Gospels give great prominence to the sorrowful mysteries of Christ. From the beginning Christian piety, especially during the Lenten devotion of the Way of the Cross, has focused on the individual moments of the Passion, realizing that here is found the culmination of the revelation of God's love and the source of our salvation. The Rosary selects certain moments from the Passion, inviting the faithful to contemplate them in their hearts and to relive them. The sequence of meditations begins with Gethsemane, where Christ experiences a moment of great anguish before the will of the Father, against which the weakness of the flesh would be tempted to rebel. There Jesus encounters all the temptations and confronts all the sins of humanity in order to say to the Father: "Not my will but yours be done" (Luke 22:42 and parallels). This "Yes" of Christ reverses the "No" of our first parents in the Garden of Eden. And the cost of this faithfulness to the Father's will is made clear in the following mysteries; by his scourging, his crowning with thorns, his carrying the Cross and his death on the Cross, the Lord is cast into the most abject suffering: Ecce homo!

This abject suffering reveals not only the love of God but also the meaning of the human person himself.

Ecce homo: *the meaning, origin and fulfillment of human person is to be found in Christ, the God who humbles himself out of love "even unto death, death on a cross" (Philippians 2:8). The sorrowful mysteries help the believer to relive the death of Jesus, to stand at the foot of the Cross beside Mary, to enter with her into the depths of God's love for humans and to experience all its life-giving power.*

"APOSTOLIC LETTER OF POPE JOHN PAUL II
ON THE MOST HOLY ROSARY:
ROSARIUM VIRGINIS MARIAE," 22

The First Sorrowful Mystery

The Agony in the Garden

They went to a place called Gethsemane; and he said to his disciples, "Sit here while I pray." He took with him Peter and James and John, and began to be distressed and agitated. And said to them, "I am deeply grieved, even to death; remain here, and keep awake." And going a little farther, he threw himself on the ground and prayed that, if it were possible, the hour might pass from him. He said, "Abba, Father, for you all things are possible; remove this cup from me; yet, not what I want, but what you want." He came and found them sleeping; and he said to Peter, "Simon, are you asleep? Could you not keep awake one hour? Keep awake and pray that you may not come into the time of trial; the spirit indeed is willing, but the flesh is weak." And again he went away and prayed, saying the same words. And once more he came and found them sleeping, for their eyes were very heavy; and they did not know what to say to him. He came a third time and said to them, "Are you still sleeping and taking your rest? Enough! The hour has come; the Son of Man is betrayed into the hands of sinners. Get up, let us be going. See, my betrayer is at hand."

MARK 14:32–42

We walk through the grove of ancient olive trees—offspring of those Jesus knew—into the large, dark, quiet basilica. Before the altar stretches an expanse of raw rock. Is this the rock washed by the sweaty blood of our Savior? Certainly this is the garden where he came for the greatest struggle of his life.

Jesus is completely human even while he is completely divine. He is the most highly sensitive of humans in his humanity and in his faith. Prophetic foresight only augmented his suffering. In the coming few hours he would undergo physical abuse beyond anything I can ever imagine. It is enough to make him sweat blood. But on top of the physical anguish there is so much more. He is a man; he wants and needs his friends. He needs human support. How densely insensitive we are. We avoid being with him in his passion and prayer in the agonies of our sisters and brothers today—if not by sleep then by unawareness, other occupations, and cultivated distractions. We do not have time to watch with him for an hour, but we have time for hours of television or chatting with friends. "Could you not watch one hour with me?" The friars at this Basilica of All Nations invite each of us to watch in union with them for one hour the first Thursday of each month as they watch here in Gethsemane with Jesus.

Horrible physical abuse, degradation, abandonment, and piercing loneliness are not the whole sum of it for Jesus; in fact, they are the least part. For this Son, who so loves to be before the Father, who so loves the Father, now stands before him with all our sin. He will be left to experience abandonment and separation from the Father. I, who have such a meager sense of what sin is, can in no way conceive of this agony.

It wrings our heart, yet comforts: The obviously depleted figure, wrung out by hours of agony, finds rest upon an angelic shoulder, comfort, and consolation.

Much lies ahead: betrayal, arrest, abandonment, brutal treatment, mockery and derision, hours of lonely suffering, abandonment, and death. But in a sense the worst is over. The "yes" has been said. The rest will in some way make sense because of the "yes."

It was not an easy "yes." Feelings, emotions, deep human urges fought against it. Death is unnatural. It tears apart body and soul. Suffering, like death, is a consequence of sin. And this is the sinless One. Death and suffering were not his due. Abandonment made them all the worse and betrayal cut deep. Sweat mysteriously turned to blood. The cry rose from deep within: If it be possible…let it pass.

All things are possible for God. Why not this? Yes, it is possible to let it pass—but love still asks for it. "Not my will, but yours." Love answers love—giving the supreme witness to love: "Greater love than this no one has than to lay down his life…."

The surrender of love brings ministering angels. We humans have failed him. We are so asleep to reality, so often not there. So often our fear turns us into cowards. "Could you not watch one hour with me?" When was the last time we watched—simply watched an hour with him?

Teresa of Jesus, the great mystic of Ávila, said she would begin her prayer by creeping through the garden until she came to the point where she could watch. And she watched. Watching suffering that says: "See how much I love you" makes great demands on us. What other response can there be than a complete "yes"? Yet we are afraid of a complete "yes." It leaves us so vulnerable. The Beloved can do whatever he wants with us. We don't trust that much. We had rather go to sleep, continue on in our half-conscious way. Alas, never knowing the ultimate ecstacy of total love, of the complete "yes" of love with its total union and communion.

The Father sent a comforting angel. Did the Hero of the agony really need such comfort? Or was the comforter sent for us and for our sake—to assure us that when we finally have the courage to pass through our own inner agony—dying to the false self—and say our "yes," comfort will be there?

What was the comforting angel like? Did this one take on human form? And allow his robe to be stained with bloody sweat? We know the human touch of comfort is important. But we know something deeper is more important: A love that says, "I am with you." Such love can reach across the miles, the continents, the oceans.

If we are indeed one with Christ through the transformation of baptism, so our sufferings are his even as his are our redemption, and his comforting is ours. The visitations of divine comfort, even if they do not take visible angelic form, are never absent from us in our distress, if we but open ourselves to them in a "yes," to the perhaps mysterious but ever-loving will of the Father. "Not my will but yours be done."

Our Father…

The Second Sorrowful Mystery
The Scourging at the Pillar

So Pilate, wishing to satisfy the crowd, released Barabbas for them; and after flogging Jesus, he handed him over to be crucified.

MARK 15:15

Jerusalem, the Chapel of the Flagellation: It is all covered now by churches and schools and other institutions. Save for some stones in the floors of the churches and in the excavations, little can be seen from Jesus' time and experience. But here, perhaps many feet or yards down, the most precious blood flowed out, stained the paving stones, seeped into some crevices, and consecrated this soil forever. Bits of sacred flesh, as sacred as that which I ate at the altar this morning, spattered about, torn out by whips of leather and bone.

That flesh and blood is honored in these buildings, hidden under sacramental veils in tabernacles of gold. The hiddenness of Christ. Hidden in pain and humiliation.

It would take a lot of courage for an artist, if he be not the most callous of persons—and then he would probably not be drawing a picture of the Savior—to bind the hands of our Lord even with ropes of pencil lead and to draw each one of his sacred wounds. It would put him excruciatingly in touch with reality.

For the reality is that we have bound the hands of the Lord, those hands that ever reach out to us in love, ever since they secretly and most lovingly fashioned us in the womb. The hands that would embrace us and heal us we tie with rough cords, lest we feel their most caring touch, our hearts melt, and we are forced to desist from our sinful ways. Our gentle artist would rather hide this painful ignominy behind our Savior's back to spare himself the pain and to spare us the painful confrontation with the doing of our obstinate self-centered love.

Nor could our gentle artist bring himself to disfigure the most holy body of his Beloved and ours with the gaping wounds that leather thongs and sharp iron tips would soon produce, each one convicting us of our heartless sinfulness. The wound of our pride. The wound of our gluttony and overindulgence. The wound of our lust and sensuality. The wound of our dishonesty and selfishness. And on and on. Our sins have never ceased, nor have they ceased to rip the body of Christ.

Here are we confronted with the lean naked body and the pleading eyes of love. Let us not mistake the pleading cry of those eyes. They do not say: Please, do not tear me to pieces. Oh, they do say that. After all he is a man, a man of flesh and blood, and his body and all his sensibility recoil from the impending agony. But more is his pleading for us, we who hold the whip, and we who have the freedom and means to scourge his most sacred body, to wound it in so many ways. His silent, loving pleading is for us—whom he loves so much. For he knows that each blow that tears his body, tears us even more profoundly. It does violence to the Body of Christ that we are. It does violence to our very nature, to the right order of the nature of one who has not only been most lovingly created as a creature of this God of love but has also and even more wondrously been baptized into the very Body of Christ.

As horrible as is the violence done to the body of our Savior by the whips of the burly Romans, as horrible as is the violence done to the Body of Christ by our sin, the greatest violence is done to our very own nature, to who we are, when we rebel against God and ourselves in sin. Or when, in our weakness, we betray ourselves and our God. Such is the love of this Man for us, the selfless love, that he suffers more from what we suffer than from what he himself suffers.

By his wounds we are healed. His sorrow-filled plea is that we do not whip him with our sin. Yet his love is such that he allows the tearing and scarring wounds of those whips to be the very healing of our sin. If only we let them be.

We need to let the reality of each of our Savior's gaping wounds be present and confront us. We do need to see that it is our hand that holds the rope that binds his loving, healing hands. Those hands for years had ceaselessly reached out in healing: lepers, the blind, the deaf, those who suffered violence—even the violence of his own chosen "pope." He only wants to reach out and touch us and heal us. But we, in so many ways, bind his healing love. We do not believe. We do not trust. We fear such love, lest it bind us even more tightly. For what other response can we give to such love, but total self-giving love?

In our selfishness and in our incomprehension we do not want to be bound by such love. We want to be "free" to do our own thing—our own shortsighted thing which we so foolishly believe to be the way to happiness. We do not understand that the only way to happiness for us is the way of self-giving love, of recklessly receiving all the love this Divine One would pour out upon us and with equal recklessness give all the love we have in return.

We hold the rope, though not with any firm determination, for his grace is in fact at work within us. We avert our eyes, lest we see his look of infinite compassion and love. It would melt us and we would immediately be converted.

As we pray this decade, let us have the courage to look into those eyes and even perceive the numinous of the Divine beyond them. Perhaps, just perhaps, we will then open to that grace, that he indeed wants to give us, that will hold back our arm so ready to strike, that will enable us to keep from inflicting any further wounds upon the One already wounded far too much. wounded for us and by us.

Our Father…

The Third Sorrowful Mystery

The Crowning With Thorns

Then the soldiers led him into the courtyard of the palace (that is, the governor's
headquarters); and they called together
the whole cohort. And they clothed him
in a purple cloak; and after twisting some
thorns into a crown, they put it on him.
And they began saluting him, "Hail, King
of the Jews!" They struck his head with a
reed, spat upon him, and knelt down in
homage to him. After mocking him, they
stripped him of the purple cloak and put
his own clothes on him.

MARK 15:16–20

Jesus suffered much here in the Praetorium,
wherein the sadistic young Roman soldiers
took Jesus in hand. He had been condemned
to death. His life was worth nothing; he was

theirs for sport. The heavy stones of the pavement still show the forms of the different games they played here to wile away the time. Little did those "playful" young men know that the one they played with that day was the very Son of God.

A big, burly, brute of a man ferociously forces the homemade crown down upon the sacred head. He does not want to get any more pricks from the vicious thorns. He has already gotten enough of them in plaiting this extraordinary crown. I wonder if ever another has worn such a crown?

With the broken pieces of reed, he forces the crown down onto the unprotected brow. The long thorns rip open the flesh, even as others force their way through the matted hair to do the same, and go deeper to press into the skull. I really cannot fathom what must have been the pain and agony that tore into this most sensitive soul. I think of the dizzying, numbing migraines I have had. And the throbbing fever headaches. But these are nothing in comparison to what this Man now suffers.

But it is not only a question of physical pain. The soldiers had heard his declaration. Their commander, the righteous Pontius Pilate, had asked, with a certain derision masking a deep fear: *Then you are a king?* And he answered with an unnerving calm dignity: *You say that I am. For this was I born and for this I have come into the world. But my kingdom is not of this world.* He is a king—the king of the despicable Jews—this naked, tattered remnant of a man. Then he shall be honored as a king. The crown was plaited. A rough red cloak was found to drape over his shoulders, already made red with blood, torn by deep, gaping gashes. A reed for a scepter was forced into his bound hands. And then the show began. Creatures dared to assail their Creator. Hands that were lovingly fashioned in the womb struck the face of the one who so lovingly fashioned them. Knees bent in derision. Disgusting spittle punctuated even more disgusting words that debased truth and turned it into mockery. King of the Jews! Yes, and Lord of all creation. I wonder, when the moment of enlightenment came for these lusty young men, in this life or in the judgment, what must have been their reaction to the almost unbelievable sacrilege that they had perpetrated?

But are they to be so completely condemned? Are they not more sinned against than sinning? We have seen it again and again. Good young men plucked from their healthy home environment, shipped off to some camp where they are trained to be vicious killers and given the weapons to do it. Then they are transported to some far distant and wholly alien post and left with hours of boring routine. The deepest sadistic tendencies emerge. And what follows is not worthy of a human person. These young Romans had known many hours of emptiness and loneliness and suffered their share of derision at the hands of the Jews. Now the king of the Jews was in their hands. He may now be a tattered remnant of a man but he looked smart enough last Sunday when he rode into Jerusalem amid the cheering and adoring crowds. Then the cloaks were going on the ground to soften the fall of his donkey's step. Branches were waving and voices shouting glad Alleluias. *Hosanna to the Son of David*. Let this Son of David see what kind of royal authority he has inherited. *Hail, King of the Jews*. The smacks resound and the spittle flies in the wake of the sacrilegious words.

Before I even think of laying any condemnation at the door of these young Romans, let me first look at my own record. I do know and confess that this is indeed the Son of David, the Son of God, the King of the Jews and my

King. Yet, the way I so frequently act, is it not a mockery of his lordship over me? Is it not a mockery when I say to Jesus: You are my Lord and my God, and then, instead of doing what he wants, I blithely go on to do just what pleases me. I allow the boring routines of my life serve as an excuse for seeking "compensating" pleasures. I give him so little of my time and attention. He who asked, *Could you not watch one hour with me?* does he get even an hour of my time each day, not to speak of a tithe? If actions speak louder than words, how genuine and authentic is my homage of him as my King and God?

What reparation can I offer to him for all that he has suffered for me and from me, for what he suffers now as these brutes crown him and mock him? I can certainly offer my many headaches and the humiliations that come my way. I can offer, too, the many unwanted thoughts and images that invade my head like so many thorns. My mind and imagination are not wholly under my control. They just keep turning out their thoughts and images, even when I wish that they be still and leave me at peace to worship and contemplate, or even simply to rest. I can develop a certain facility to let much of the constant mental chatter and shadow go by. But there are the painful thoughts and images that come to renew old pain and humiliation. They wring my soul again. And the thoughts that provoked that hatred and anger which I do not want. I do want to forgive and forget. I have forgiven. But the inner computer still holds the data and it mercilessly keeps coming up. And there is the lust, too, that would betray me and lead me to use others, betraying their openness and trust. Lord, have mercy. I am truly pierced by these thorns, and so many others. May your piercing be my healing. May my suffering and the offering I make of it in union with your crowning make some reparation to you for all you have suffered for me. May I grow in compassion for you and for all your suffering members. Even for these young Romans, and all who through the centuries, even to our own times, have had their own humanity so abused that they have become abusers. Help me, O Lord, to work and pray for total disarmament of mind and heart, of home and nation, until all this abuse ends.

Lord, I stand, I kneel, in true homage, before you, my Lord and King. I worship you and hail you as the true King of the Jews (May your people come to recognize and worship you!) and of us all. You have paid such a price because of all our pretensions, you the true King. Lord, have mercy.

Our Father…

The Fourth Sorrowful Mystery

The Carrying of the Cross

As they led him away, they seized a man, Simon of Cyrene, who was coming from the country, and they laid the cross on him, and made him carry it behind Jesus. A great number of the people followed him, and among them were women who were beating their breasts and wailing for him. But Jesus turned to them and said, "Daughters of Jerusalem, do not weep for me, but weep for yourselves and for your children. For the days are surely coming when they will say, 'Blessed are the barren, and the wombs that never bore, and the breasts that never nursed.' Then they will begin to say to the mountains, 'Fall on us'; and to the hills, 'Cover us.' For if they do this when the wood is green, what will happen when it is dry?"

> Two others also, who were criminals,
> were led away to be put to death with him.

LUKE 23:26–32

Jerusalem, the *Via Dolorosa*: The artistic and rather antiseptic tableaux in our churches prepare us not at all for the experience of making the stations of the cross in Jerusalem. Here they are totally immersed in life. The judgment takes place in what is now a Muslim schoolyard. The journey wends down narrow, shop-lined streets along the north and then the west side of the Temple area before striking off up Golgotha. Some stations are marked by little chapels set in the respective buildings; others are but a mark on the wall. As we make our way along, life goes on as usual. Shops are busy; merchants try to sell us all sorts of religious trinkets and many other things. Children rush about us in their games. Older Muslims and Jews belligerently push their way through our praying throng. Some make rude noises, but most simply ignore us.

And so it was when Jesus first made this journey. Curiosity caused some to stop and look as the criminals were led out. But most took little notice while the Son of God went forth to die for them. A few friends and a crowd of dedicated enemies followed. A stranger was forced to help, carrying the heavy cross—too heavy now for a man who has been so brutalized (even if he *is* God).

How happy I would be to help Jesus carry his cross, to have the divine eyes rest upon me, to receive that look so full of love and compassion. Indeed I envy the Cyrenian.

But what were the dispositions of his mind and heart? Was he in some way a disciple? Did he realize what a privilege was his? Did he perhaps at that moment when the divine gaze rested upon him receive some enlightenment, like the good thief upon the cross? Or was he so filled with self-pity at having been dragged into this thing that he totally missed the grace of it? Was he so humiliated at being publicly identified with this poor wreck of a man, this public criminal, that he could think of nothing but himself?

There were others, of course, who entered into the drama of this sorrowful journey. John, the beloved disciple, was never very far away. His love compelled him to stay as close as he could, right to the end. Perhaps it was he who brought the virgin Mother. What a dreadful moment of encounter that was when first the divine gaze met the eyes of his mother. Once Jesus said to one of his saints: If I had not made the world, I would make it just for you. He would certainly have said to Mary: If I did not need to die for anyone else, I would willingly die for you alone. But perhaps the greatest sorrow of his whole passion, after the crushing pain of standing before his Father with the guilt of all our sin, was for him seeing the pain and anguish in the eyes of his most dear mother. He willingly suffered to keep her free from all sin and all the consequences of sin. Yet in that same love he could not deny her the longing of a mother's heart to be with her son in his most bitter agony. How mysteriously are love and suffering woven together by compassion—in the deepest meaning of that word.

There were other women, too. The courageous one whom we call Veronica, who pressed through the crowd and even pushed her way past the rough and burly guards to give a moment of refreshment to the Victim far more refreshing because of the love it expressed than any physical comfort it afforded. The courageous kindness was rewarded so wondrously, a reward we have shared through the centuries: a true icon, the very image of our suffering Savior.

And those other women, less courageous, yet nonetheless courageous enough to publicly show where their feelings lay. They received the compassion of a mysterious prophecy that would perhaps someday comfort them or the children they now held in their arms.

But it was a man—and I am not quite sure what exactly that is meant to say to us—who was allowed to enter most fully into Christ's most painful and wretched journey. Maybe it says that we less sensitive men need to be touched more physically by the pain of the Lord in order to respond and be with him in compassion. Maybe it intimates something about our role in the ongoing work of the redemption, of making the saving passion of Christ present in the world today. I can only think of how horrible must have been the pain our Lord was suffering as that heavy beam pressed down and lurched back and forth on those shoulders lacerated with innumerable open and burning wounds. To be able to lift off some of that burden, if not all of it, even for part of the horrendous journey! Such an intimate, powerful, and poignant call to compassion, to *be with* our Beloved in his *passion*.

As I survey the scene from a safe distance my heart is deeply moved and there is a deep longing to be with the Lord, to be Simon the Cyrenian, to have the unique and immense privilege of helping our Lord carry his cross. And yet what happens when the distance is closed, when that cross is offered to me in my own daily life? Are my eyes of faith quickly blinded by my wallowing self-pity? Am I so humiliated and self-conscious that I lose all consciousness of the privilege that is being offered me? Do I totally forget that we are indeed called to *make up what is wanting in the passion of Christ?*

The first time I heard those words in the epistle of Saint Paul I wondered about them. What could be wanting in the passion of Christ? It was more than complete. It had satisfied for all our sin and more. What could be wanting in the passion of Christ? The mystery of it—that God wants the passion of Christ to be effectively present in our world today by our participation in it. Ours is the privilege, a costly one—as costly as it is sublime—to make Christ's passion and all its healing effects present to our brothers and sisters. And to ourselves, here and now by our living that passion in ourselves, by being like Jesus a complete "yes" to whatever the Father asks of us. "Yes" even when our human nature, like his, sweats blood and cries to be let off.

If I can only clearly see and keep in mind that the headache and the heartache that I am asked to bear with today is my opportunity to be Simon, to actually help Jesus carry his cross, to be intimately with Jesus in his passion—how much easier or, at least, more meaningful will be each of my daily crosses. May this be part of the grace that is woven into my life, into my consciousness, as I pray again and again this fourth sorrowful mystery.

Our Father…

The Fifth Sorrowful Mystery
The Crucifixion

And they [the soldiers] offered him wine mixed with myrrh; but he did not take it. And they crucified him, and divided his clothes among them, casting lots to decide what each should take.

It was nine o'clock in the morning when they crucified him. The inscription of the charge against him read, "The King of the Jews." And with him they crucified two bandits, one on his right and one on his left. Those who passed by derided him, shaking their heads and saying, "Aha! You who would destroy the temple and build it in three days, save yourself, and come down from the cross!" In the same way the chief priests, along with the scribes, were also mocking him among themselves and saying, "He saved others; he cannot save himself. Let the Messiah, the King of Israel, come down from the cross now, so that we may see and believe." Those who were crucified with him also taunted him.

When it was noon, darkness came over the whole land until three in the afternoon. At three o'clock Jesus cried out with a loud voice, "Eloi, Eloi, lema sabachthani?" which means, "My God, my God, why have you forsaken me?" When some of the bystanders heard it, they said, "Listen, he is calling for Elijah." And someone ran, filled a sponge with sour wine, put it on a stick, and gave it to him to drink, saying, "Wait, let us see whether Elijah will come to take him down." Then Jesus gave a loud cry and breathed his last. And the curtain of the temple was torn in two, from top to bottom. Now when the centurion, who stood facing him, saw that in this way he breathed his last, he said, "Truly this man was God's Son!"

There were also women looking on from a distance; among them were Mary Magdalene, and Mary the mother of James the younger and of Joses, and Salome. These used to follow him and provided for him when he was in Galilee; and there were many other women who had come up with him to Jerusalem.

MARK 15:23–41

Calvary! The narrow steps are steep. It is a dark corner in the vast Basilica of Saint Savior, the Church of the Holy Sepulcher. Like everything else in Christendom, it is divided: half Roman Catholic, half Greek Orthodox.

Chants from a multitude of liturgies in a multitude of languages drift up from all parts of the Church of the Holy Sepulcher to form a sonorous cacophony. Hundreds of lamps bring the frescoes, mosaics, and gold-covered icons to life. On a bench near the railing a man sleeps peacefully, stretched out under a blanket. No one disturbs him. An Orthodox nun with an entourage from the women's auxiliary busily renews the lamps. A sleepy young Franciscan yawns and scratches as he awaits the end of a mass that an elderly Spaniard is celebrating with great fervor. Old women wearing black dresses and kerchiefs repeatedly prostrate themselves and then crawl under the altar to reach down and touch the actual stone of Calvary.

Should Calvary be like this? Perhaps so. After all, the passion of Christ was and is totally enmeshed in life, although our pictures and images too often set it apart. Christ's passion is the very center, the culmination, the summit of all creation, because it is the summit of human and divine love. Yet it is within *all* aspects of creation—even the lowliest. It is the leaven that raises up, that makes all capable of being loved and worthy of the Father.

I stand here with John, the disciple whom Jesus loved, feeling helpless. There is a time for doing. And a time for being. And a time for being with. The three hours must have seemed an endless eternity—three hours standing at this spot, watching Jesus hang here, life flowing out, each breath more labored. There is nothing to do but let Jesus suffer and give all for us. This is difficult.

Jesus asks in prophetic voice: Has there ever been a sorrow like unto my sorrow? And we must answer: Indeed, no. As we look upon him who has been pierced, what can we say?

This exquisitely beautiful body, the fruit of a virginal womb, of a sinless one, untouched by the blight of human sin, never has a body been more sensitive to pain. And now it is elongated in crucifixion, gasping for every breath. Every muscle already exhausted, yet it must strain for another gulp of air. And with each exertion the gaping wounds in wrist and feet wear and tear yet more around the cutting, rough iron of the nails. Flailed by more wounds than any can count as they crisscross one another, shredding the tender flesh. The mockery of the crown, emphasized by the sign overhead, King of the Jews, brings its own throbbing pain and piercing torture as the head is thrown back again and again in spasm against the rough wood. And the humiliation of his nakedness, exposing the very fragility of his manhood.

Beyond this is the deeper pain, that of the sinless one clothed in all sin. No human has ever comprehended the full malice of human sin, but this man-God. And knowing that malice, he stands before God, his Father, with the whole crushing weight of it upon him. No one has ever loved the Father as has this beloved Son. His love is the very person of the most Holy Spirit of Love. Yet that love is violated by all sin, now his sin. *Father, if it be possible, let this chalice pass from me.* If it be possible. Certainly it was possible. But love still asked. And love still gave.

No, there never has been any sorrow like unto this sorrow. And yet no artist dare try to depict it in all its horror. If one should dare to attempt it the picture would immediately be labeled garish or crude. Yes, it is crude, horribly crude, what has been done to this man.

And we are confronted by it. It is time to leave off words. Rational analysis, images—what can they do but belittle it. It is beyond all these. We can only contemplate the reality, opening ourselves to the intuitions of Divine Love, allowing love to bring us beyond ourselves to experience that which transforms even if it is too much to inform—too much beyond our human receptive capacities to receive form.

As we allow this reality to be a presence within us, the Crucified Christ, we come to see its reflections, its shadows, its participated reality in the world all around us. We see the Crucified One in the despised African American whose humanity the arrogance of the White keeps nailed down. We see the Crucified One in the "lazy Indian" whose humanity has been truncated and numbed by a subhuman, corralled environment. We see the Crucified One in the "licentious gay" whose humanity, labeled and libeled and unaccepted by family, society, and church, cries out in its loneliness for compassion and relationship. We see the Crucified One in the ghettoized Jew who is set outside the city and the society by some distorted "Christian" instinct. We see the Crucified One in the disabled, who are not given a chance to reveal their true inner beauty and to use the splendid talents they do have from the Lord. We see the Crucified One in all the suffering, the despised, the segregated. We see, if we have eyes to see.

The longer we look upon him who has been pierced, the humbler we become. We come to know the leprosy of our own sin; how despicable we ourselves indeed are. We come to know we are one with the despised and crucified Christ and by his wounds we are healed. We come to know that we are in truth one with every wounded human, we are all wounded. We come to know *compassion*, we "suffer with." And there is no one whom we do not "suffer with."

We have moved with Christ through his mysteries, from his descent and self-emptying at the Incarnation, through his gestational and educational experiences, to the bloody steps of his passion. Now it is time to stop. To be. To leave off the parameters of our own thoughts and images. To be before the cross, wide open. And to let ourselves be invaded by the Divine in their most powerful expression of their compassion.

This fifth sorrowful mystery is indeed, the mystery for contemplation.

Our Father...

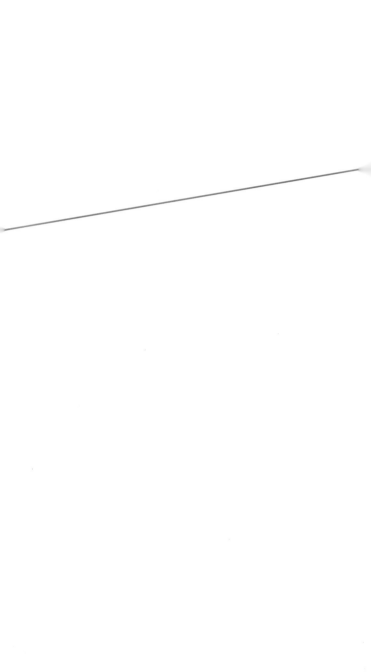

The Five
Glorious
Mysteries

The contemplation of Christ's face cannot stop at the image of the Crucified One. He is the Risen One! The Rosary has always expressed this knowledge born of faith and invited the believer to pass beyond the darkness of the Passion in order to gaze upon Christ's glory in the Resurrection and Ascension. The glorious mysteries thus lead the faithful to greater hope for the eschatological goal towards which they journey as members of the pilgrim People of God in history. This can only impel them to bear courageous witness to that "good news" which gives meaning to their entire existence.

"APOSTOLIC LETTER OF POPE JOHN PAUL II
ON THE MOST HOLY ROSARY:
ROSARIUM VIRGINIS MARIAE," 23

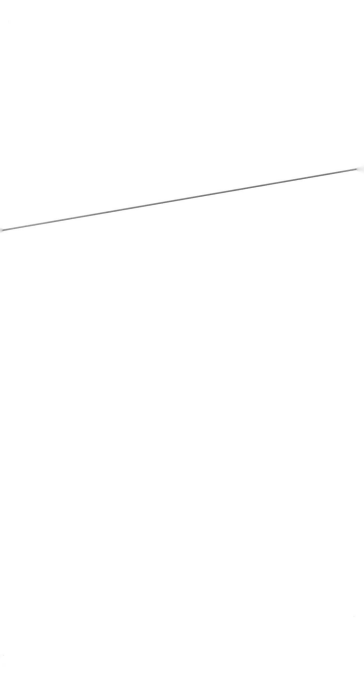

The First Glorious Mystery

The Resurrection

When the sabbath was over, Mary Magdalene, and Mary the mother of James, and Salome bought spices, so that they might go and anoint him. And very early on the first day of the week, when the sun had risen, they went to the tomb. They had been saying to one another, "Who will roll away the stone for us from the entrance to the tomb?" When they looked up, they saw that the stone, which was very large, had already been rolled back. As they entered the tomb, they saw a young man, dressed in a white robe, sitting on the right side; and they were alarmed. But he said to them, "Do not be alarmed; you are looking for Jesus of Nazareth, who was crucified. He has been raised; he is not here. Look, there is the place they laid him. But go, tell his disciples and Peter that he is going ahead of you to Galilee; there you will see him, just as he told you." So they went out and fled from the tomb, for terror and amazement had seized them; and they said nothing to anyone, for they were afraid.

Now after he rose early on the first day of the week, he appeared first to Mary Magdalene, from whom he had cast out seven demons. She went out and told those who had been with him, while they were mourning and weeping. But when they heard that he was alive and had been seen by her, they would not believe it.

MARK 16:1–11

I n the Church of the Holy Sepulcher, the great bell booms with such intensity that the whole basilica seems to vibrate. The different hierarchs are arriving for the great feast, each with his own procession of clerics and faithful. The liturgies will go on all morning, sending up their collective (and, sad to say, competitive) chants to the Throne of Mercy. What strikes me most strongly in this great, multilayered church is that the center is not

Calvary but this empty tomb—this empty tomb that is the very center of Christian faith. "If Christ has not been raised, your faith is pointless."

But he *has* been raised. The tomb is empty. One after another, priests and nuns, women and men, people of all ages, bend low and enter the dimly lighted chamber. They kneel and kiss the stone. Little attention is paid to the icons and frescoes. No, it is the emptiness that matters. He is not here. He is risen.

Christ has risen. Christ has truly risen. And he has not risen only for himself alone nor alone. Saint Matthew tells us in his gospel that when Christ died tombs were opened and the bodies of many saints rose from the dead, and these, after his resurrection appeared to many people (see 27:52–53). Pope John XXIII, sitting upon his throne in his cathedral church of Saint John Lateran, literally *ex cathedra*, told us that it can piously be believed that Joseph, the husband of Christ's virgin Mother, was among these holy people and that they ascended with him into the heavenly places.

In the traditional icons of the early Church we see Jesus, having "descended into hell," raise up Adam and Eve and lead them forth. Here our artist leaves us with a bit of ambiguity. There is but one pair of hands that grasp the liberating hand of the triumphant Savior. Is it Adam? Is it Eve? The fact is that in the Lord there is neither male nor female. Both have been resumed in their fullness. The risen Christ, into whom each one of us has been baptized—we were buried with Christ in the waters of baptism and rose up out of them into his risen life— calls us forth to the fullness of human life with its complete integration. He reaches to draw forth from us all the repressed dimensions of our being, to call us to live a full life in him. Again "the glory of God is the human person fully alive."

He is fully alive and all glorious, this risen Savior of ours. Yet we see unmistakably in his hand and in his foot, the mark of the nails. Not now grizzly, gaping wounds but rather glorious marks of victory. A great victory over sin and death, over the most sacrilegious of crimes, the most base of human deeds.

We see in ourselves the ravages of sin. If we do not die a young and sudden death, we will mark the diminishments that move us inexorably toward dissolution. Jesus allowed to be worked in his most perfect and sinless body all the ravages lusty and cruel people could work. He was totally wrecked until finally his very heart was pierced and the last drops of blood and water flowed forth. Thus he witnesses to the supreme power of his resurrection, as he rises all glorious and triumphant. Because he has risen, we too shall rise. *If he be not risen our faith is in vain.* But he is risen. And we shall rise. No matter what our sins and the sins of our parents and our people have wreaked in us, we too shall rise all glorious and beautiful. And what we have suffered for Christ and for others—*whatever you do for the least of my brethren, you do for*—me will leave its marks upon us, not disfiguring marks but marks of yet greater glory.

As we face the diminishments of life we want often to pray this decade and meditate on this mystery. In it is our sure hope and our confidence. For even now, our risen Lord reaches to us to raise us up in spirit and to make our faces shine with his joy and his peace. This is the beauty we saw in the face of a Mother Teresa, that face so worn and furrowed with countless wrinkles yet compellingly attractive. This is the twinkle we saw in the eyes of John XXIII, the old man who knew many years of exile but ended up "on the top of the heap" with enough vigor to change the history of humankind. This is the light of the resurrection that would shine out of each one of us if we would but die to all the pretenses of our false self and simply be who we truly are—men and women baptized into the risen Christ, who has conquered death and all the effects of sin and stands before us, reaching out to us, with wounds all glorious. Let us reach out and clasp his hand in loving and trusting faith.

Our Father…

The Second Glorious Mystery

The Ascension

So when they had come together, they asked him, "Lord, is this the time when you will restore the kingdom to Israel?" He replied, "It is not for you to know the times or periods that the Father has set by his own authority. But you will receive power when the Holy Spirit has come upon you; and you will be my witnesses in Jerusalem, in all Judea and Samaria, and to the ends of the earth." When he had said this, as they were watching, he was lifted up, and a cloud took him out of their sight. While he was going and they were gazing up toward heaven, suddenly two men in white robes stood by them. They said, "Men of Galilee, why do you stand looking up toward heaven? This Jesus, who has been taken up from you into heaven, will come in the same way as you saw him go into heaven."

Then they returned to Jerusalem from
the mount called Olivet, which is near
Jerusalem, a sabbath day's journey away.
When they had entered the city, they
went to the room upstairs where they
were staying, Peter, and John, and James,
and Andrew, Philip and Thomas,
Bartholomew and Matthew, James son of
Alphaeus, and Simon the Zealot, and
Judas son of James.

ACTS OF THE APOSTLES 1:6–13

Again, emptiness. The climb up Olivet
is long and hot. We pass through the
olive groves, then pass the Church of All
Nations and the many-domed Russian Church
of Saint Mary Magdalene. The teardrop chapel
that marks the spot where Jesus wept over
his city is set in a green oasis amid thousands
of graves. Finally at the summit, we enter a
low door and come to the plain stone dome
that stands over the spot from which Jesus
traditionally is said to have ascended. The
little chapel, the Church of the Ascension
in Jerusalem, is totally bare. Here, as elsewhere,

the Muslims took over a site sacred to Jesus' memory, stripped it of all icons and frescoes, of all the rich Byzantine art, and then used it as a mosque. The minaret they built still stands by the entrance to the courtyard, a great circle within which stands the totally empty church. Emptiness. Plenty of space to imagine how it might have occurred.

I imagine that there was something of a twinkle in the Lord's eye. He can hardly keep from smiling. Here he is sending off this motley crew of cowards, telling them to go forth and teach all nations. It was like the time he met Peter and called him "Rock"—the man who would quail before the questioning of a little servant girl. Yes, he chose the weak of this world, so that no flesh would glory in itself. Peter would become rock but only after he finally got in touch with his own weakness and his love. He had done a lot of stupid things; he had really failed his Lord. And he had wept. Now he was ready. And so were the others, more or less.

They still dreamed dreams: Lord, will you establish your kingdom at this time? Yes, they still saw themselves lording it over others in this world's fashion. They had not heard him declare to Pilate: My *kingdom is not of this world.*

For now, all they needed to do was to go into the city and wait for the Holy Spirit. The Paraclete, the Comforter, the Strengthener, the one who would make them strong and recall to their minds all he had taught them, would come to them ten days hence. They needed a retreat. They needed to reestablish their number, finding a replacement for poor Judas. They needed to gather around Mary, the Mother of the Church, and prepare for its birth—its birth in them. For that mystical Spouse who sacramentally came forth from his side on Calvary's hill, came forth in blood and water, was to actually come forth in them on Pentecost.

But they do not quite understand all this yet. They do not understand the share in his chalice that is to be theirs. So they stand here, clinging to him, if not physically like the women at Easter, certainly and more tenaciously in their hope and fear and, yes, love. They have come to love him very much, just as he loves them. *No longer servants, but friends.* This separation is difficult, but it is necessary. *If I do not go away the Spirit cannot come.* If everything is centered on the physical presence of Christ in one place, the mystical Body animated by the Spirit cannot grow and reach out to all the corners of the earth. The mission of the Head on earth is complete, now it is time for the Body to be formed by the Spirit. And these men, this motley crew are to be the primary agents of the Spirit. These men and their apostolic successors are to head the Body on earth until it is complete and ready to ascend to be one with its Head in the eternal kingdom and glory of the Father.

Jesus has completed his mission on earth. He has lost none of those whom the Father has given him except that son of perdition. Now it is time for him to depart.

He has given his charge. He smiles. He blesses. And he quietly ascends. The apostles had seen many things. He had one day walked into each of their lives. He had called them. And they had responded. Though perhaps none of them could really say why. Certainly they had no idea what their response was going to lead to. He so often just disappeared from them. They learned to let that be. He wanted to have those nights alone with his Father. And he returned, sometimes even walking on the water or walking along a country road or walking through a closed door.

But now his going was different. They followed him with loving and longing eyes as he serenely ascended. There was a certain definitiveness about this departure. And there was something deep within each one of them that wanted to go with him, to ascend to where he ascended. He had promised: *I go to prepare a place for you.* But not now. For now, they had a mission. *Men of Galilee, why do you stand here looking up to the heavens?*

There is something deep in the heart of each one of us that stands, looking up to the heavens. We are, indeed, made for the heavenly kingdom. And we have been promised, we too, that a place is prepared for us. If we let go of all the superficial little wants to which we give much too much attention, we will come to be in touch with this great longing. And we will come to know that it can begin to be fulfilled, even now, as we turn within. *The kingdom of God is within.* And we will also come to realize that the way to its complete fulfillment is to be found in our now seeking to fulfill the will of God in our lives. God is where his will is. We must leave off at times our contemplation of heavenly things to go into the city and do what the Lord wants us to do. But may we never loose touch with the desire that is deep within us for Christ, to follow him into the heavenly kingdom. May we always have the desire to stand here in the idleness of contemplation, looking up to heaven. May this second glorious mystery bring us back here again and again.

Our Father…

The Third Glorious Mystery

The Descent
of the Holy Spirit

When the day of Pentecost had come, they were all together in one place. And suddenly from heaven there came a sound like the rush of a violent wind, and it filled the entire house where they were sitting. Divided tongues, as of fire, appeared among them, and a tongue rested on each of them. All of them were filled with the Holy Spirit and began to speak in other languages, as the Spirit gave them ability.

Now there were devout Jews from every nation under heaven living in Jerusalem. And at this sound the crowd gathered and was bewildered, because each one heard them speaking in the native language of each. Amazed and astonished, they asked, "Are not all these who are speaking Galileans? And how is it that we hear, each of us, in our own native language? Parthians, Medes, Elamites, and residents of Mesopotamia, Judea and Cappadocia, Pontus and Asia, Phrygia and Pamphylia, Egypt and the parts of Libya belonging to Cyrene, and visitors from Rome, both Jews and proselytes, Cretans and Arabs—in our own languages we hear them speaking about God's deeds of power." All were amazed and perplexed, saying to one another, "What does this mean?" But others sneered and said, "They are filled with new wine."

But Peter, standing with the eleven, raised his voice and addressed them, "Men of Judea and all who live in Jerusalem, let this be known to you, and listen to what I say. Indeed, these are not drunk, as you suppose, for it is only nine o'clock in the morning. No, this is what was spoken through the prophet Joel:

'In the last days it will be,
    God declares,
that I will pour out my Spirit
    upon all flesh,

and your sons and your
daughters shall prophesy,
and your young men shall
see visions,
and your old men shall
dream dreams.
Even upon my slaves, both men
and women,
in those days I will pour out
my Spirit;
and they shall prophesy.
And I will show portents in the
heaven above
and signs on the earth below,
blood, and fire, and
smoky mist.
The sun shall be turned to
darkness
and the moon to blood,
before the coming of the Lord's
great and glorious day.
Then everyone who calls on the
name of the Lord shall
be saved.'"

ACTS OF THE APOSTLES 2:1–21

✤

Once a church, later a mosque with its niche toward Mecca, now just an empty upper room. Emptiness again. Emptiness, crying for fullness. This space has been transformed many times, but perhaps these are the very walls that trembled under the onslaught of a mighty wind as the Holy Spirit transformed her trembling little Church into the powerful missionary force that could obey the departing command of its Founder: go forth and teach all nations. The command has not yet been completely fulfilled. The same Holy Spirit comes upon each of us—at baptism, at confirmation, and each day that we welcome her—and empowers us to use the Christ we are. She empowers us, as she did him who went forth from the Father, to go forth and proclaim, by the way we live as well as in our words, the good news that Jesus is Lord, risen from the dead.

God can never be deceived. Nor will he ever deceive, for he is, indeed, Truth itself. This is the ground of our faith.

God became man in Christ—Christ, the Way, the Truth, and Life. Before he completed his earthly mission and ascended to his kingdom, Jesus promised his Twelve that Holy Spirit, his Spirit, the Paraclete, the Comforter, Love would come upon them not many days hence. They were to go to Jerusalem to await her.

The Twelve understood now more clearly that they had a mission: Go forth and teach all nations, baptizing them in the name of the Father and of the Son and of Holy Spirit. As they gathered in the upper room awaiting the Paraclete, they were not the timorous little group who huddled there fifty days earlier, filled with sorrow, confusion, and pain. They were not exactly sure what Jesus' promise meant, just who this Holy Spirit was and how she would appear or come to them. But they believed. They had a mission. They rounded out their number, choosing a successor for Judas. They waited. Many came to wait with them. And in their midst, as an inspiring and steadying force was Mary, their life, their sweetness, and their hope. They prayed.

The Spirit came, came in power. And the Spirit came as one might have expected: in a mighty wind and fire. All the great theophanies of old were being fulfilled. The Lord, who descended upon Sinai in lightning and thunder, filling his people with awe and fear, made a covenant with them. Now a new covenant was established, a covenant written in God's own blood, shed on another mount, that of Calvary. The church that was born from the side of Christ on Calvary was now inspirited. The church came forth to the world, to peoples of every nation, gathered together by divine design here at Jerusalem.

As the mighty wind embraced the house and shook it to its very foundations, tongues of fire came to rest upon the head of each. Each received Holy Spirit. And each in his or her own way.

A new and almost fierce determination shown in the eyes of Peter. He was now ready to lead the Lord's little band forth to become a worldwide community of believers. The Rock was now rock, solid, firm, strong—no more cowardly denials would mar his total fidelity. Without hesitation he stepped forth, silenced the immense crowd gathering around the house, and spoke with power. He needed the help of the rest of the Twelve to baptize the thousands who came forth. Peter always needs the others to help him in his ministry.

James was no longer a "Son of Thunder." As the Spirit came upon him he went within to find a new peace and wholeness. He was to be the first of the twelve to drink the "cup" which the Master had drunk. His preparation for that had begun.

For his brother John it was another experience. He received the Love of his Beloved, this disciple whom Jesus loved. And he understood, as only the Spirit can make us understand, the secrets of Love: That the second command is like unto the first, that we are to love our neighbor as ourself. Not "love our neighbor as if she or he were ourself." No, our neighbor is ourself, we are truly one in Christ. When we fail to love our neighbor, we fail to love ourself. And conversely, if we do not love ourself, we cannot love our neighbor. In fact, there is only one Christ loving himself.

This is why we need deep prayer, that quiet contemplative prayer where we see ourselves reflected back to us in the eyes of our God who so loves us. Only then do we see our own tremendous beauty and begin to love ourselves as we deserve. And at the same time we see that in this creative divine Love we are, indeed, one with all. We see the beauty of all. We love all as ourself.

At this moment John also understood that other secret of love which Jesus had taught them:

Whatever you do to the least of my brethren, you do to me. Again, the oneness. And John rejoiced that he could still do something for his Beloved. He went on to spend the rest of his long life doing just that. Above all and before all, he sought to share the secrets of love. "Little children," the old man repeated again and again, "little children, love one another."

Our God of love never ceases to pour out his Love. Each time we pray this decade we open our hearts to receive that outpouring, one with the whole Church, which we are. And each time, each of us receives that Spirit of Love in the particular way that is appropriate to us and to where we are right now on our journey. We have but to open wide our hearts in waiting and expectant love, like the apostles, with Mary.

Our Father…

The Fourth Glorious Mystery

The Assumption of Mary

My beloved speaks and says to me:
"Arise, my love, my fair one,
    and come away;
for now the winter is past,
    the rain is over and gone.
The flowers appear on the earth;
    the time of singing has come,
and the voice of the turtledove
    is heard in our land.
The fig tree puts forth its figs,
    and the vines are in blossom;
    they give forth fragrance.
Arise, my love, my fair one,
    and come away...."
Come with me from Lebanon,
        my bride;
    come with me from Lebanon.
Depart from the peak of Amana,
    from the peak of Senir and
        Hermon,

from the dens of lions,
from the mountains of leopards.

You have ravished my heart, my
sister, my bride,
you have ravished my heart with
a glance of your eyes,
with one jewel of your necklace.
How sweet is your love, my sister,
my bride!
how much better is your love
than wine,
and the fragrance of your oils
than any spice!

SONG OF SOLOMON 2:10–13; 4:8–10

This is one of the most peaceful and quiet places in the Holy City of Jerusalem—actually, it is just outside the Zion Gate of the Old City—the crypt of the great abbatial church of Dormition Abbey, which crowns the summit of Mount Zion. Here, according to tradition, was the house where Mary dwelt after Jesus' Ascension until her own blessed death. It is just around the corner from the cenacle and a short walk from Calvary and other places now filled with sacred memories for the Holy Virgin.

There is a peacefulness in this deep crypt that is most appropriate. The exquisitely serene figure of Mary that lies in repose at the center of the crypt invites us to deeper peace.

On Calvary Mary was given a weighty responsibility to mother John and all of us—to mother the whole Church. She was with the infant Church in the fear-filled days after the Ascension, leading the small but growing community in prayer. After the fearful ones were empowered by Holy Spirit, Mary's task was easier. But until the end she was the mother-presence within the Church at Jerusalem.

Sometime before the cruel and bitter days of the sixties, Mary completed her earthly ministry and went to sleep in the Lord—only, like her Son, to be quickly awakened. No eyewitness saw his rising, though he appeared to many later. And no eyewitness beheld his mother's resurrection, though she has frequently appeared through the centuries.

Mary was raised up and carried on high by the love of the One who rose and ascended on high. Like Son, like mother. All of us who have been baptized have been baptized into the death and resurrection and ascension of Christ. He is the Firstborn from the dead. We follow, by his powerful love. And first among us followers was Mary.

If Christ has not been raised, our faith is in vain. But Christ *has* been raised. Our faith is *not* in vain. And the Most Faithful One first experienced the fulfillment of her faith and love. We all shall follow.

She is most special.

Come, then, my beloved, my lovely one, come.

Whether Mary, like her sinless Son, experienced death or not, we do not know. The theologians argue this way and that. When Pope Pius XII solemnly proclaimed Mary's Assumption, he was careful not to decide the question. The Scriptures are silent. We do not know. We do not need to know. What we do know is that, once Mary had completed her mission on earth, her Son sent his holy angels to bring this sacred ark of the new covenant, the body from which he received his body, to immediately share the glory of his own resurrected body.

Could this Son, himself preserved from corruption, ever allow his mother, the Holy Virgin, to see corruption? Could he allow her most pure flesh from which he drew his own flesh, this body ever preserved as a most sacred temple, the ark of the new covenant, could he allow something so sacred to know the ultimate effect of sin? Could he allow death to celebrate its complete victory over her?

Everything in us says "No."

What son of a most loving mother would ever allow his mother to descend into the grave and know mortal decay if he had it in his power to keep her at his side in radiant beauty? Already Jesus had known sorrow enough in the pain he had caused his mother as he went forward to his divinely appointed mission. Leaving her alone in her widowhood, faced with the recriminations of uncomprehending relatives, was hard enough. Allowing her to walk with him to Calvary and to stand by his most torturous deathbed, a cruel consolation he could not deny her, cost him more than it cost her. Even if it was not due her, even if his filial duty did not demand it, the loving heart of this Son could hardly have borne to allow her to lie in corruption while he enjoyed all the bliss of the heavenly kingdom.

He could not let his holy Mother see corruption. He could not allow the woman he loved most in all creation be anything but most beautiful. He had completed all the sorrows and pains of his mission. His heart was to be pained no more. Their separation, even in the flesh, had lasted long enough. Now that her mission was also complete, she was to be at his side in glory. She who had so valiantly stood by his cross would sit on his throne, just as close in glory as she had been in ignominy.

We who love Mary can only rejoice in this. We who know her as Mother want nothing less for her. We are happy that her Son has the power and the goodness to glorify her and to glorify her without delay. And we cry: *Look down from the heights....* Even as you enjoy the glory of your Son and with him prepare a place for us, help us to come to that place.

The glory of the mother is the glory of her children. Mary's glory is Christ's glory. And it is our glory and our hope.

Our Father...

The Fifth Glorious Mystery

The Crowning of Mary

A great portent appeared in heaven: a woman clothed with the sun, with the moon under her feet, and on her head a crown of twelve stars. She was pregnant and was crying out in birthpangs, in the agony of giving birth. Then another portent appeared in heaven: a great red dragon, with seven heads and ten horns, and seven diadems on his heads. His tail swept down a third of the stars of heaven and threw them to the earth. Then the dragon stood before the woman who was about to bear a child, so that he might devour her child as soon as it was born. And she gave birth to a son, a male child, who is to rule all the nations with a rod of iron. But her child was snatched away and taken to God and to his throne; and the woman fled into the wilderness, where she has a place prepared by God, so that there she can be nourished for one thousand two hundred sixty days.

And war broke out in heaven; Michael and his angels fought against the dragon. The dragon and his angels fought back, but they were defeated, and there was no longer any place for them in heaven. The great dragon was thrown down, that ancient serpent, who is called the Devil and Satan, the deceiver of the whole world—he was thrown down to the earth, and his angels were thrown down with him.

Then I heard a loud voice in heaven, proclaiming,

"Now have come the salvation and
        the power
    and the kingdom of our God
    and the authority of his
        Messiah,
for the accuser of our comrades
        has been thrown down,
    who accuses them day and night
        before our God.
But they have conquered him by
        the blood of the Lamb

and by the word of their
testimony,
for they did not cling to life even in
the face of death.
Rejoice then, you heavens
and those who dwell in them!
But woe to the earth and the sea,
for the devil has come down
to you
with great wrath,
because he knows that his time
is short!"

So when the dragon saw that he had been thrown down to the earth, he pursued the woman who had given birth to the male child. But the woman was given the two wings of the great eagle, so that she could fly from the serpent into the wilderness, to her place where she is nourished for a time, and times, and half a time. Then from his mouth the serpent poured water like a river after the woman, to sweep her away with the flood. But the earth came to the help of the woman; it opened its mouth and swallowed the river that the dragon had poured from his mouth. Then

the dragon was angry with the woman,
and went off to make war on the rest of
her children, those who keep the com-
mandments of God and hold the testimony of Jesus.

REVELATION 12:1–17

We are heading toward forty thousand
feet in a clear, blue sky high above the
Mediterranean. This is probably the closest I
will get—for a while—to the site of the coronation of Mary as Queen of Heaven and Earth.

As Israel recedes, I wonder what thoughts
Mary might have had as the angels bore her aloft
for her coronation. Was it so swiftly done that
there was little time for thought? Was Mary so
lifted up in expectation that she had little
thought for what was below? "Forgetting what
is behind, press forward toward the mark."

Hardly like a mother. Yes, she was eager to
lay eyes again on her Firstborn. But he is the
Firstborn of many brothers and sisters. Mary
loved the Body of her Son, the little Church,
rapidly expanding, seeking to fulfill his final
words: "Go forth and teach all nations."

In one sense Mary had fulfilled her most special vocation. It had cost her far more than any poor human heart can comprehend. She had willingly paid the price in full, given all that God asked of her, suffered as only a mother can suffer for her child. Mary certainly earned the merited crown that now awaited her in the heavens. The entire choir of the kingdom was there to joyfully welcome her. Her ancestors, so proud, were there. Her own mother rejoiced in acknowledgment of a motherhood that made her the grandmother of God and made her daughter God's dearest.

Yet it was in the ecstatic love that impelled Mary into the very heart of the Trinity that she held in deepest maternal care each and every member of her Son—a care that is as real and effective today as it was on that day of assumption and coronation over 1,900 years ago. In the very "now" of God it is all one.

It is good—it is awesome—that the most exalted of all women, the gloriously crowned Queen of Heaven and Earth, right this moment and always holds me in her maternal love. With such care, how well I fare. I certainly need never despair. It is a mother's love and care that help hold my childish pettiness and stupid narcissism within limits. A mother's care from a mother who has given us proof of limitless love and care.

I lift my eyes from my own needs. I can leave them in her care. I scan the blue vault that domes the endless fields of clouds. It seems to open to me; I can in some way enter into the joy and exaltation of the heavenly court that celebrates the holy mother of God. It is time to join the unending chorus of the ages: *Ave, Maria, gratia plena. Dominus tecum. Benedicta tu in mulieribus.* Hail, Mary, full of grace. The Lord is with you. Blessed are you among women. Blessed above all creation. You yourself are the crown of all creation, our soiled nature's solitary boast. Our queen, our mother, the glory of Jerusalem—the heavenly Jerusalem as well as that of earth.

From all eternity God had prepared Mary for him. And now she kneels before him. Kneels, bends the knee—for he is God, albeit man; and she is a creature, a product of his creative power, albeit the most beautiful and magnificent of all his creations, a creation worthy of the divine creative energies, a creation so far beyond anything any other creature can perceive or conceive, that she fairly seems to enter within the very borders of the Trinity itself.

She kneels, so graciously, so demurely—she is the very incarnation of humility. But only for a moment, until the divine hands which had fashioned her and given her all else, bestow upon her crowning glory: the crown of the Queen of Heaven and Earth, the crown of all creation, the crown of the consort of God. And then Christ raises her up, to sit with himself on his throne.

One of my favorite mosaics in all the world is to be found in a twelfth-century church in the deeply impoverished section of Rome known as Trastevere. Santa Maria in Cosmeden was built when for the first time a Cistercian monk sat on the Throne of the Fisherman. And he was a holy man, too, Blessed Eugene III. This mosaic is unique in that it pictures Jesus and Mary together; but not Jesus as a child or Jesus at Cana or Jesus in his Passion. But Jesus enthroned in glory. And there is Mary sitting at his side, sharing his throne. *And he has his arm around her!*

Mary has been tenderly and lovingly brought into a full sharing in her Son's reign over the creation he has redeemed. This should not surprise us. Did not God promise even to us poor sinners that we who open to Jesus' gentle knock, allowing his redeeming presence and love to flow into our lives, will be given the victory and will sit with him on his throne even as he sits with his Father on his Father's throne? (see Revelation 3). No one ever so completely opened to him as this woman who gave him her body and blood from which to fashion his very human flesh and blood—the flesh and blood that would be sacrificed on Calvary and would feed us all in daily Eucharist.

Mary's sitting on that throne beside her son is no empty honor. He could never give such a model to the race he had redeemed. Woman is no mere adjunct to man, an ornament to complete the scene. Woman is a true equal, created to be man's helpmate, *like unto himself*. Jesus reigns as the Son of Man, a true man like unto us in all but sin. And he needs his woman at his side, receiving dominion, even as he does as man, from the Divine, albeit in a different way and through his mediation.

Mary participates fully in the reign of Christ, her Son. She is truly Queen of heaven and earth, of all creation. She has truly queenly power. And God has made her truly worthy of it and capable of exercising it.

The wondrous thing in this—for us—is that

this woman, the pinnacle of God's created ones, the glory of all his creation, is our mother. And even in her sublime dignity and beauty and power, she bears within her bosom all the sentiments of a mother toward each one of us whom she bore in such anguish on Calvary's hill. Can a mother ever forget the child of her womb? Not this mother. In all her sublimity she yet regards each of us as her most dear child and cares for us most tenderly, even though she does not hesitate to use the fullness of her queenly power in our behalf.

As we behold the demure, all-beautiful, and untainted one present herself before the throne of Divine Grace to be crowned and raised to sit on that throne, we can wonder what we poor sinners, so stained with sin, have in common with our tainted nature's solitary boast. She is almost too young, too fair, too beautiful, to be a mother. Yet she is mother, his mother and ours. And in all her sublimity that fact never ceases to be and to be most profoundly operative in all that she does.

We hail the Queen, knowing that she is mother, the mother of Mercy. And our mother—our life, our sweetness, and our hope.

Our Father…